The Snuff Takers Ephemeris®

THE JOURNAL OF FINE TOBACCO

Volume Seven

Winter 2012

© 2012, Lucien Publishing.

THE SNUFF TAKER'S EPHEMERIS is published quarterly by Lucien Publishing, Fayetteville NC. Volume Seven, December 2012. Cost: 10.99/single volume; 43.96/per year. Address: PO Box 287, Spring Lake, NC 28390. www.STephemeris.com.

Advertising and distribution/bulk purchase/retail queries:
distribution@STephemeris.com.

ISBN-13: 978-0-9854781-3-1

ISBN-10: 0985478136

EPHEMERIS STAFF

EDITORS

RW Hubbard
President, Publisher

Mick Hellwig
Editor-in-Chief

Micah Rimel
Managing Editor

WRITERS

Gillian Bromley

Catherine DeMarsh

Seth Desjardins

Anthony Haddad

Simon Handelsman

Mick Hellwig

RW Hubbard

Bill Johnson

Nigel McCarren

Micah Rimel

David Thigpen

James Walter

Larry Waters

PHOTOGRAPHY

Elisha Cozine
(Chief Photographer)

Natalie Spaulding

Lynn Hodges

MODELS

Jordyn Ballentine

Britney Coughlin

Jen

Lillia Luster

Divina Lynn

Mariah Taylor

....plus a bunch of others that never got back to us with their info...

Contents

SPECIAL THANKS, ACKNOWLEDGEME-NTS, AND GREETINGS

MATT SLATE

DAVE (MR. SNUFF)

RODERICK (TOQUE)

CONNY ANDERSSON (GN)

BRANT COMSTOCK

SAMANTHA BYRD

RICHARD STARKS, WUAW FM 88.3

EVERYONE AT SWEDISH MATCH

EVERYONE AT V2

THE STAFF AND READERSHIP OF THE STE

G. Inness 1866

George Inness's "Christmas Eve," also known as "Winter Moonlight", 1866.

Inness (1825-94), often called "the father of American landscape painting," was a deeply spiritual follower of Emanuel Swedenborg and felt that his art was a living manifestation of the beauty of God's creation. He also loved "coarse, bronze" French snuff, which he used for nearly thirty years.

He died in Scotland after witnessing a particularly magnificent sunset. "My God! Oh, how beautiful!" he exclaimed as he fell to the ground.

This particular piece is one of his best known works. A lonely pilgrim walks a moonlit path, while the chill of winter

NOTE FROM THE PRESIDENT

I'm mad. No, not about the election results. I could really care less about that.

I'm mad at my local tobacco shop. See, I went in there today for a couple of items and next to me in line is a teenager, no older than 15 or 16, buying a pack of Newports and some Zig Zag blunt wraps. I wasn't mad at the kid. Hell, I can count on one hand the number of times I was carded buying tobacco during my teen years. But it was a different time then, and the rules have changed quite a bit since I bought my first illegal pack of Marlboros.

The kid walked out of the store and hopped into a Monte Carlo full of stoned high-schoolers. I looked at the woman behind the counter, who was acting as if nothing had happened.

"You know that kid was underage, right?"

"No," she said. "I carded him the other day and he was 18."

"Bullshit. I'm not here to bust you, I just want to buy some snus. I'm just wondering why you sold it to him." She sighed. "He's my neighbor's kid. I know him. He's not hurting anyone."

"True," I said, "but you're hurting me." I could tell she was confused and more than a little angry. "See, everytime the ALE or ATF busts somebody like you doing exactly what you just did, they put the screws on me and every other adult tobacco user who has to answer for every store clerk like you that gets caught doing something stupid."

"How?" She asked. "I'm the one that would get the damn fine. And it's almost five grand plus community service hours!"

"Then you're doubly stupid," I said. Her face was getting redder than a sunburned alcoholic. "The Anti crowd gets a hold of an isolated incident like that and they use it as fodder to convince the government that stores like this shouldn't be selling single cigars, or that they should be taxed mercilessly to discourage children from buying them. People like you are part of the reason this can of Flader in my hand has 50% of its lid covered with an untrue statement from the Surgeon General."

But I wasn't done yet. "Once upon a time, a tobacconist was a respected member of society. Now the trade is full of people like you who wouldn't know the difference between a Macanudo and Macaroni." She opened her mouth to say something but I cut her off. "Shut up." I grabbed my stuff and walked out.

The moral of the story? There is none. But if you catch a woman selling tobacco to teens, lecture the hell out of her, tell her to shut up, and walk out of the store and take your business elsewhere. Otherwise, enjoy this issue!

RW Hubbard

Mexico.

That's where I've been for the last couple of months. Mexico is a strange country. Everyone smokes. Anything. In the poorest, most decrepit areas, they'll pull leaves off of a tree and smoke it. Families pass around giant cigars and they suck it down like marijuana blunts, inhaling the smoke as deep as they can until they can't hold it any longer.

Manufactured cigarettes are hard to come by. It's difficult to determine whether they're counterfeit or genuine most of the time. Street urchins carry boxes of "Cuban" cigar brands like Montecristo and Cohiba and try to pass them off to yankees for 20 or 30 dollars a box. Marlboro cartons are about 10 bucks a pop. They look pretty similar to real Marlboros, except the red printing on the package is more of a pinkish color. (I understand that red is is an expensive ink, so it's probably watered down by the printers to save money.)

Everywhere I went, I gave away snuff. I showed the people how to use it, and told them how to make it. They were intrigued by the thought of grinding down cigarette tobacco and adding their own ingredients. (Mexicans love to cook, if you didn't already know this.) I felt like Johnny Snuffleseed, spreading the good word of smokeless tobacco to any and all I could reach.

Will Mexico one day become a Mecca of snuff use? I don't know. But (hint hint) I believe that it could become a major player in the international smokeless tobacco market, on par with India, if the right people were to go down and invest in the local communities and attempt to start a business. Why not take advantage of NAFTA and give it a shot? The current administration in the US seems hell-bent on driving new tobacco manufacturers out of production before they even grow their first batch, so it would be more economically feasible for someone to set up shop in Juarez and import the stuff north, where it could be sold at a massive profit. A snuff cartel, if you will.

They say not to drink the water in Mexico. I say, don't smoke the Cohibas.

Ole!

Jim Walter

Dudes,

1. The sixth volume of STE really goes over the accepted BSQ (Bull Shit Quotient) with the insistence that almost every vampire movie actor was a snuffer of some sort. It's really too much.

2. I realize that STE is not an academic journal, but I did not expect it to be a tobacco version of *The Onion*. There is enough snuff history and snuff lore and old snuff humor, both American and Old World to keep you busy for a while.

3. And what's the bit with the Motörhead section and the half nekkid chick? I'd rather read about Gid Tanner and his Skillet-Lickers and see pictures of Lily Langtry. (**Ed: we almost ran a bio of Lily since she was close friends with Ed. Burne-Jones, but we couldn't confirm that she was a snuffer, although it's pretty likely.**)

4. You did have a nice photo of Theda Bara, though.

Dave Payton

Dear Dave,

1. What part of our horror movie actor/snuffer list was bullshit? I agree that 75% of each issue of the STE is composed primarily of bullshit, but I figured a 20 page article comprising years of collective research not only by the four authors who worked on it but dozens of outside sources wouldn't qualify as bullshit. Which actor(s) do you believe we misrepresented? Or is the sheer quantity too much to swallow?

I wish we had known this before we spent all the time and effort that went into the article. Next time we'll just throw darts at old issues of Famous Monsters *and pick an actor at random and write a couple of paragraphs about him or her being a snuffer, since that's basically what you're implying we did. Of course, we'll have to ignore the articles that mention their snuff habits, but you get what I'm saying.*

2. We agree. There's so much snuff history and snuff lore

out there that we try to do articles like the one you just blasted. I guess you're implying that you want us to reprint the same stuff that every other snuff book or website has ever published instead of our own original research? Again, this is just fine with me, since it means that all we have to do is copy & paste whatever we can find in a google search instead of flying across the country to interview a guy who owns a snuffbox that was previously owned by both Bela Lugosi AND Boris Karloff.

If you're comparing our non-serious snippets to The Onion, *then (as Nicolas Cage would say) that's high praise indeed. We get compared to them (and* Mad Magazine*) quite often, but we're still waiting for a* National Lampoon *comparison. Or maybe you're saying that since we're NOT an academic journal, we shouldn't be taken seriously? (Look out BMJ!)*

What exactly is *an academic journal? Wikipedia says it's:*

"A peer-reviewed **[Check]** *periodical* **[Check]** *in which scholarship relating to a particular academic discipline is published.* **[Since several colleges teach tobacciana either as a horticultural subject or as part of a cultural study, then Check.]** *Academic journals serve as forums for the introduction and presentation for scrutiny of new research, and the critique of existing research.* **[Check, and as per your letter, double Check.]** *Content typically takes the form of articles presenting original research, review articles, and book reviews.* **[Check.]"**

So holy jeez, according to the internet, we're a full-fledged academic journal. Maybe if we started labeling ourselves as such, people will take us more seriously and stop calling our research "bullshit." On the other hand, we prefer the term "sleaze rag" and rather our readers have fun reading our goofy periodical. But since we keep a circulation of six copies and we're funded primarily by homeless charities, I guess we'll never fully abandon that academic journal "spirit."

3. We have no idea how the half-nekkid chick showed up in the magazine. We were interviewing Motörhead, then BAM! - ho's was ur'rywhere. I blame Lemmy.

4. Thank you.

To whom it may concern;

I'm having great difficulty locating your magazine in any of my local bookstores. The Barnes and Nobel nearest me says they can't even stock it, but they special order it for me anyway. I don't mind ordering from the website, but I love being able to walk into a bookstore and buying directly from the shelf.

Thanks,
Paul Murphy

Paul, we love doing the same. We're freely available to all Barnes & Noble stores (and pretty much every other book or tobacco store to boot) but it's entirely up to that particular store's periodical manager whether or not he or she wants to stock our book. We recommend harassing the hell out of them until they stock us.

It's also possible that it may just be misplaced on the shelf somewhere. I went in to my own B&N the other day expecting to see Volume VI *right between* Rural Living *and* Weed World *like our last issue, but I instead found it next to the model train collectors magazines. I wish we had more control over that sort of thing, but we don't.*

Speaking of rural weed smokers:

So... Now that Obama's president again, are you guys going to kill yourselves or what?

Bernie
Via Youtube

Actually, we love Obama. Without the FDA Control Act, SCHIP, or PACT, we wouldn't have had anything to bitch about for the last four years.

Dear STE,

Was the letter from the guy in the newest issue [*about Christianity and King James' sexuality, Volume VI*] for real? I have a hard time believing that there's someone out there that retarded or that he reads the same magazine as me. Please say it was a joke.

Cameron Phillips

Unfortunately Cameron, the letter was indeed genuine. But don't call the writer "retarded"; that's just not PC anymore. Use the term "mentally dumb" instead.

Dearest STE,

I know you've stated numerous times on the forums that you have no intention of reprinting the first four issues. But consider this. I started with Volume 4 and I'm missing the first three. I even printed out the digital copies and stapled them together but it just wasn't the same. Please, please PLEASE reprint the first few issues at some point. I work all day at a computer screen and the last thing I want to do when I get home is pick up a Kindle or a tablet to read your magazine.

Love,
Lana Mushey

Hopefully you've heard by now about our Master Series collection, which will reprint Volumes 1-4 in our current format with a ton of bonus material. This way you'll have a nice matching set of STE's for your shelf and you'll get to see some behind-the-scenes stuff too.

The Master Series won't be available in brick and mortar bookstores, but you'll find them online at the usual places like Amazon, Barnes & Nobel and our own site, www.STEphemeris.com.

Letter of the Month

Guys,

I got a postcard thru the mail the other day and it reminded me of the Edgar Cayce snuff can predictions (*Volume V*). Maybe this guy knows more about the snuff prophecies. Just look at his face, he seems so... prophetic!

James Milner
Sandy Eggo, California

He's certainly a dour enough looking chap. The back of the card claims that his psychic prowess helped return five kidnapped US contractors in the Middle East. It also states that he works under numerous pseudonyms "for the necessary peace and quiet" that he needs to help benefit the people with his psychic powers. Oh, and if you send him some money, he'll send you winning lottery numbers. What a swell guy.

For turning in this awesome piece of nonsense, we'll in turn send you a whole year's *worth of nonsense: a four issue subscription to the STE. Also, if you send us some money, we'll send you some winning telephone numbers.*

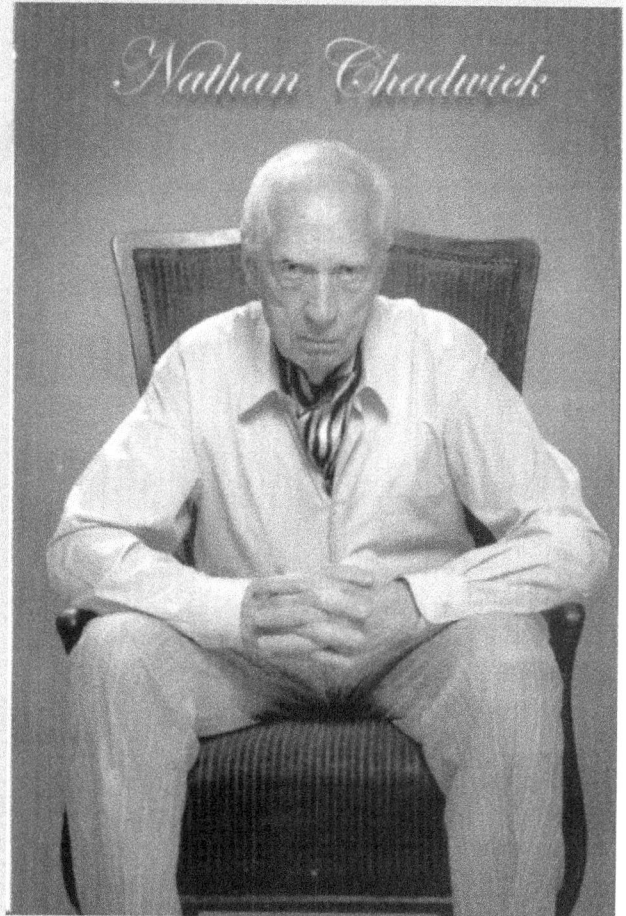

Psychic Seer Ray Walston, er, Nathan Chadwick

Hello,

I just got volume six in the mail today and I'm extremely excited. I'm also working my way through back issues. I bought and read the digital copy of volume one and plan to buy the rest either in digital or print (hopefully) form. I enjoyed Volume One so much that I had to get Six in print as soon as I could and I knew I wouldn't be disappointed. It's a beautiful magazine and I hope I can help it continue circulation by purchasing and letting as many people know about it as I can.

I did have one idea. In addition to being a snuff and snus user/lover/advocate, I am also a huge fan of podcasts. I listen to podcasts six to eight hours a day while at work and in my free time and its a great way for people with boring or repetitive jobs to be entertained. I don't think there are many tobacco related podcasts and I think the people at STE would be the ones to make a great one. Even if they were only quarterly supplements to the magazine. Not that I want you guys to have even more on your plate than you already do. Just a thought.

That aside I wanted to sincerely thank everyone at STE for a great publication that I look forward to having on my bookshelf for a long time. I mean heck, there is a large tribute to Bela freakin' Lugosi in this volume. Now *that* puts a big smile on my face. I know I'm babbling but I just appreciate people putting hard work into things that they love. Thank you very much to the entire STE Staff and contributors.

Sincerely,
Clay J. Sizemore

P.S. Sorry for rambling.

Don't apologize for rambling. After all, this is The Ephemeris, *where each article rambles on for at least two pages past its optimal ending point.*

The podcast sounds like a great idea. Hopefully we'll eventually have the time to put one together.

Dear STE,

Just wanted to say that I think the Bela Lugosi article(s) were the best thing you've printed to date in the STE. And the filmography/stageography was probably the most concise I've ever seen- all the more astounding since it came out of a magazine like STE and not one of the genre magazines like *Midnight Marquee* or *Screem*.

Paul Mazarsky,
Ohio

Thank you Paul! We've been working on the Bela tribute for over a year now, and we're glad that it was so well-received.

We did the filmographies especially for the nitpickers (like me) that have yet to see a concise Lugosi film listing in print. We tried to ensure that it was as accurate as possible, but we know that there may be some errors in there, lurking...

Hello all,

As a female reader of your book, I decided I would share my thoughts regarding the new "sexy" Ephemeris that you introduced with the new issue. I loved it! The models in the main magazine were all very pretty, and the slutty little "Monster Metal Megazine" was dead on. As a metal kid of the 80's, it was a perfect parody of every headbanging *Circus* or *Metal Edge* magazine we teens used to devour. Keep it up!

Natalie Patrick
Orange, SC

Hey Natalie, if you like the magazine so much, why don't you send us some naked pictures of yourself? Then we'll REALLY like you.

If you stop running the naked girls in future issues, I'll still buy your magazine but I won't enjoy it as much.

"Teraz"

Neither would we.

Hi,

As a lesbian reader of your magazine, I say keep running the girls. The last "spread" was a little tacky, but the rest of the pictures were amazing.

"Name Withheld"

Thanks, NW. The MMM shoot was supposed to be over-the-top, tacky, extreme- everything you'd expect from a piece involving Motörhead. I think most of our readers understood that we weren't trying to be Playboy, we just had some fun with the source material.

That's not to say we're against running nudes in the magazine. Did you know that in Australia, Volume VI was sold in a plastic bag to people over 18 only? It makes me feel good knowing we're in such pleasant company as Swank, Hawk, Juggs, Oui, Rustler, Cheri, Club, Barely Legal, Tight, Leg Show *and* Black Tail.

STE

This issue dedicated to Chief Frank Brown of the Canupawakpa Tribe (Dakota Nation, Manitoba Canada)

Manitoba, Canada- When Chiefs Frank Brown and Orville Smoke were ordered to shut down their tobacco shop near Pipestone, they agreed. As soon as the Police left the shop, the two men (along with store manager Garth Blacksmith) re-opened the store and continued selling their tobacco.

Four subsequent raids were carried out, each time resulting in the RCMP confiscating all tobacco from the store. Within hours, the shelves were re-stocked and the store opened back up for business. The store was shut down each time for failure to carry the proper permits to sell tobacco and refusal to charge or remit sales tax on goods bought from the shop.

Located in the southwestern part of the Manitoba Province and named after the legendary "Catlinite" clay that was used by North American Indian tribes for two millennia in the construction of their tobacco pipes, the area is home to many remaining Native Americans, including the Dakota nation which includes the Canupawakpa tribe. The Dakotas have attempted to reclaim land that has belonged to them for approximately a thousand years, though the Royal Government refuses to sign a treaty that formally recognizes them and grants them the same land rights and benefits as other North American tribes.

Chief Brown sees the cat-and-mouse tobacco shop shenanigans as a sort of peaceful protest. "I am not a Canadian, I am a Dakota," he said during the initial hearings. Justice Brenda Keyser then upped his fine from $1500 to over $10,000. Brown showed no emotion. "I'm not going to pay it. They can put me in jail. I just don't care."

Brown, Smoke and Blacksmith were then charged with Contempt of Court, which typically carries a six month sentence. Chief Smoke's charges were dropped and his fines waived when he publicly distanced himself from the store and announced that he wanted no part of the "controversy."

Chief Franklin Brown.

Other members of the Dakota tribe have not been so quick to turn tail, however. Over forty tribesmen arrived on horseback at the Winnipeg courthouse on November Fifth in a show of support for Brown and Blacksmith. The spectacle attracted the media, but it failed to sway the courts, who seized the business and claimed it for the Province.

Many Indigenous People's civil rights groups have stepped up in support of Brown. Some have even threatened to barricade federal oil and water pipelines that run through Dakota land if Chief Brown is jailed. The pipelines funnel oil from treaty-granted land that the Indians receive no compensation for. Chief Ray Brown (no relation) summed it up thusly: "Canada has taken our land, our water, our oil and now our businesses and they don't want to give us anything in return. Our tribe has a 90% unemployment rate because our farms and businesses have been reappropriated for the Crown. I ask, how much more do they want?"

Most of the Canadian Dakotas have long since crossed the border into the US, to be reunited with their fellow tribesmen who have (for the most part) not had their treaties with the state of Minnesota dishonored. Let's hope Canada steps up to the plate and offers the same recognition that the US has shown to this historically peaceful and patient tribe.

Ephemera!

Study Finds New Yorkers Most Likely To Avoid Tobacco Taxes Altogether

With some of the highest tobacco taxes in the nation, it should come to no surprise that most tobacco users in New York are getting their products somewhere else.

The **South Bronx Litter Pack Survey Study** analyzed approximately 1000 discarded tobacco containers, mostly cigarette packs. Of these empty packages, 76.2% avoided the combined New York City and State tax. 59% of these were untaxed altogether, meaning they were purchased on Native American reservations, bought on the black market, or were foreign counterfeits being passed off for genuine brands.

Only 19.4% of the packages indicated that all required taxes were paid. 4.4% of the packages were too badly damaged to analyze adequately.

If this study is indicative of New York City tobacco users on the whole, then that means that 8 out of 10 tobacco users are avoiding the crippling taxes by purchasing their tobacco on the grey or black markets.

When informed of this flagrant violation of NY tax code, King Bloomberg flew into one of his characteristic childish rages. All attempts to calm him down were unsuccessful, until a staff member turned on a Spongebob DVD and sat Bloomberg down in front of it with a bowl of ice cream.

Study: Snus more effective at long term nicotine absorption than cigarettes, nicotine gum

Although the study carried out by the center for Nicotine and Tobacco research didn't reveal any startling new facts regarding the efficiency of snus in satisfying a user's nicotine needs, it was the first time that various strengths of snus were pitted head to head with cigarettes and nicotine gum.

Between the three products, test subjects on the whole absorbed more nicotine from gum than snus or cigarettes. However, absorption from cigarettes was almost instantaneous yet had the shortest halflife of the three products.

Snus users absorbed nicotine the slowest, yet after an hour the nicotine in their system was highest of all three products, reinforcing the idea that snus is the most effective at curbing the need to smoke. It was also found that snusers who used lös or high-nicotine portioned snus consumed less tobacco overall compared to users of traditional strength snus.

Good job, Legacy Foundation and Tobacco Free Kids!

The CDC reported that tobacco use among high school students in the US dropped 2.6% between 2009 and 2011.

Though this number is statistically insignificant in every way possible, some anti-tobacco groups are using it to take credit for helping to curb the epidemic of teenage tobacco use. We wish them well in their continued delusional endeavors.

... collecting all the news that's fit to reprint

Nicotine increases intelligence, fights Alzheimer's

The University of Amsterdam is standing behind their controversial study that indicates nicotine enhances learning capability and memory retention. This was especially true in the elderly; since comprehension and memory are key areas of loss in Alzheimer's patients, researchers tested nicotine patches on elderly people with Alzheimer's, and found that **after regular nicotine doses, they were two times faster and significantly more consistent** at answering memory-based questions than the control group.

Anti-tobacco activists have protested for years against the use of nicotine-based medication in the fight against Alzheimer's, schizophrenia and attention deficit disorder, despite proven evidence that nicotine is an effective and safe drug when used to treat those disorders. Now that increased mental capacity has been added to the list of positive things that nicotine can do to the human body, these same activists are outraged.

"These idiots need to calm down," according to a press release by a joint committee calling itself **"The Ghosts of Dead Geniuses Who Used Tobacco,"** which includes such expired luminaries as Galileo, Darwin, Newton, Einstein, Carl Sagan, Margaret Mead, Sigmund Freud, and Thomas Edison, among others. "In this world," stated Committee Speaker **Ghost of Benjamin Franklin**, "Nothing in life can be said to be certain but death, and that tobacco can make you a genius. I think all of us here prove my observation to be correct. Also, another sure thing is that there's always going to be some a-hole jealous of your intelligence, and will therefore try to **tax you down** to his level of stupidity. The world grows stupider as it turns away from tobacco. Hence television programs like *Jersey Shore* and *Honey Boo Boo*." Spectral Albert Einstein also chimed in to explain that Stephen Hawking has been waiting to join their group for the last fifty years, so that he could once again hold a pipe to his lips. "He won't quit screwing around with that damned wheelchair, though," Spectral Einstein sighed.

"This is exactly what I warned against," claimed an exasperated and disembodied Charles Darwin, between pinches of snuff. *"People of today are too stupid to understand my* **Origin of Species**, *so they completely overlook the main point of the book: that the less tobacco we, as a society, consume, the more ape-like and barbaric we will become. 19% of Americans use tobacco. 70% of the Chinese use it. Guess who owns who."*

BELOW: DARWIN'S THEORY OF DE-EVOLUTION OF NON-SMOKING MAN.

The Electronic Cigarette Industry Trade Association (ECITA) has responded formally to the "leaked" EU initiative that would ban the sale of all smokeless tobacco products, including electronic cigarettes. (Read Larry Water's definitive article last issue for more information.)

In a letter to the European Commission, ECITA president Katherine Devlin said: "As we understand it, the Commission will now have completed the Impact Assessment for this consultation process. This will no doubt have indicated the significant economic growth of the electronic cigarette industry, and your own Eurobarometer survey clearly demonstrates how significant the positive impact on public health could be, if electronic cigarettes remain widely available to smokers.

"It is crucial that the proper regulatory standards are in place, but this cannot be achieved through medicinal regulation. The costs are too high, and the restrictions on the flexibility and appeal of the product are too great, so all the considerable public health benefit potential would be lost."

As with most trade industry queries about the proposed smokeless ban, this one has also gone unanswered by the EU committee.

Alternative Tobacco Products becoming a broader category in convenience stores

During the August Convenience Industry Outlook Forums, Don Longo claimed that OTP (*Other Tobacco Products* such as smokeless, dissolvables and e-cigs) is now the sixth largest convenience store sales item.

According to Longo, Editor-in-Chief for *Convenience Store News*, smokeless tobacco product sales increased by 6.3 percent in 2011 from 2010, and should grow at least 6 percent by the end of 2012. A 12 percent increase in two years is an astronomical growth rate for a tobacco category that critics have called "dead in the water."

The biggest growth segment in the category has been electronic cigarettes, whose year-to-date (YTD) dollar sales increased by 221 percent over last year and are projected to grow by 138.7 percent for 2012. Overall sales could exceed $1 billion by 2015, he said. According to the CSNews 2012 Industry Report, 2011 average sales per store for e-cigarettes were up 535 percent.

"Increased availability, longer duration on shelves and, to a lesser extent, the addition of more brands per store are driving E-cig sales," Longo said. "Most of the top e-cig brands have seen astronomical growth, led by NJOY and Logic Technologies."

The dollar share of the category for the first six months of 2012 was smokeless (including snus) 69 %; cigars, 24% but trending downward; pipe/cigarette tobacco, 3%; e-cigarettes, 2%; and rolling papers, 2%.

Snus use not linked with acute myocardial infarction

In yet another study (this one by the Division of Public Health & Epidemiology at the Karolinska Institute in Stockholm), snus is again shown to be the safest tobacco product available.

According to the study, long term snus users are at no higher risk for a myocardial infarction (also known as a heart attack) than people who have never used tobacco before. Anti-tobacco extremists have since been busy trying to come up with a way to discredit their findings. If the anti-smokeless crowd ends up making a complete ass of itself (as it usually does,) we'll be sure to print their hilarious lies and speculation for the entertainment and whimsy of our readership.

Smokeless Manufactures in India Protest Government Ban on Guthka With A Series of Controversial Ads

Now that Guthka (Indian oral snuff) has been banned in 14 states, an industry coalition of smokeless tobacco manufacturers have shot back with a series of sarcastic, taunting ads aimed directly at the government.

In one of the ads, a set of lungs blackened with tar and cancer are compared with a clean set of healthy lungs. "This is how our government wants you to die," is printed underneath the black lungs. "This is how we want you to live" is printed underneath the clean lungs. A bidi cigarette is pictured over the black lungs next to the word "LEGAL" while a can of Guthka is pictured next to the word "ILLEGAL" beside the healthy lungs.

Other ads are similar in tone, questioning the hypocritical ban on less-lethal Guthka while far more dangerous smoking tobacco remains legal. Many of the ads cite studies and statistics that show how much more dangerous smoking is compared to smokeless use.

While public opinion seems to be in favor of the tobacco manufacturers, government officials are enraged by the ad campaign, calling it "deadly propaganda." A recent ad shot back urging the public not to believe the government's "dangerous misinformation" along with the urging to "save your health, and your life. Stop smoking and switch to smokeless."

These pro-smokeless ads have angered anti-tobacco activists as well, who claim that the ads are a flagrant violation of the government ban on any and all tobacco advertising. "Such ads undermine and demean the gutka ban and are in clear violation of Section 5 of the Cigarettes and Other Tobacco Products Act, 2003," said a spokeswoman from a children's health advocacy group.

The controversy has perhaps influenced the Delhi High Court to "temporarily ignore" the state government's decision that imposes a blanket ban on gutka products, which is good news for Indian snuffers and snuff manufacturers.

Phillip Morris gives up the fight against Norwegian tobacco display ban

PMI's Norwegian unit, Phillip Morris Norge, has decided to drop its appeal of the government law that bans tobacco products from being displayed out in the open.

In Norway, all tobacco products are kept behind and under the counter or in another room completely invisible to the consumer, who must ask for the product by name. PMI argued that the law hindered trade of legal products and failed to document the health benefits justifying such a hindrance, but the Oslo supreme court upheld the law, claiming that it "benefited the health of the public" and so superceded any free trade laws.

Though it has the opportunity to further appeal the decision, Phillip Morris has decided to accept the Oslo defeat for reasons unknown. A spokesman for Philip Morris Norge refused to say why the company had decided not to appeal the city court ruling, calling its analysis of the ruling "internal information."

Perhaps PMI just doesn't have the same hypocritical backhandedness that Phillip Morris North America displayed by going along with the PACT and FDA tobacco acts, which pundits have dubbed "The Marlboro Preservation Act" since it places strain on PM's competition while Phillip Morris NA remains relatively unscathed. Maybe if we send over some of our sleazy American tobacco execs, Norway will once again be able to market legal tobacco products to adults.

Until then, smokeless tobacco users in Norway are reportedly working on a set of X-ray glasses that will allow them to see through the wooden counter and peruse the various brands at their disposal. We wish them success.

Pfizer Attempting to Stall Chantix Lawsuit

ALABAMA- Pfizer Inc., the pharmaceutical company behind the ineffective stop-smoking aid Chantix, is attempting to delay proceedings in the class action lawsuit against them. 2600 separate lawsuits have been filed against the New York-based company by families and victims of Chantix users who experienced disastrous side-effects caused by the drug; mainly suicide and mental breakdowns.

Chantix, which has less than a 2% rate of effectiveness in permanently keeping smokers from ever smoking again, has long been known for its tragic side effects that can cause a person to suffer a mental or nervous breakdown and in extreme cases, lead a user to commit suicide.

Pfizer asked a federal judge to delay the trial "to allow all parties to complete discovery and any pre-trial motion practice" related to "new clinical data."

In addition to preparing its defense, Pfizer is trying to keep its chief executive, Ian Read, out of the courtroom. A U.S. District Court judge has permitted Mr. Read to testify as a witness in the trial, but Pfizer last week appealed the decision, arguing his appearance would be burdensome and unnecessary. An appellate court decision is pending.

Meanwhile, the FDA is still urging smokers to switch to pharmaceutical NRTs such as Chantix, which are much more dangerous than snuff or snus and 1/5th as effective as smokeless tobacco in keeping smokers off cigarettes.

...and on that note...

CKRA (Central Kentucky Research Associates) are paying teen tobacco users a cool 800 bucks to take part in clinical studies of Chantix, despite the proven risk of suicide and other dangerous side effects outlined in the lawsuit above. Guess who's funding the project? (We'll give you a hint- it's Pfizer.)

So if you have a smart-assed nephew aged 12-16 and want to see him learn a lesson at the end of a rope or by OD'ing on pills, sign him up at **http://www.ckraresearch.com/2012/01/adolescent-smoking-cessation-3/** and let the hilarity ensue.

...but wait, there's more!

The American Cancer Society's John Sefferin falsely announced that tobacco would kill "up to a billion people this century," while urging people to switch to pharmaceutical alternatives like Chantix and Nicorette. (Pfizer, in an **amazing** coincidence, just happens to donate millions of dollars a year to the ACS.)

Sefferin has shown himself to be a damned liar on numerous occasions. Whether it's misquoting published reports or skewing studies to fit his prejudiced agenda, Sefferin has proven himself adept at taking the money and running off at the mouth. Let's hope that American smokers ignore his plea to avoid smokeless tobacco as a means to quit cigarettes. Maybe then we can save those billion future victims...

Article by Pete Munro; Originally Published by the Sunday Morning Herald, *10-15-12*

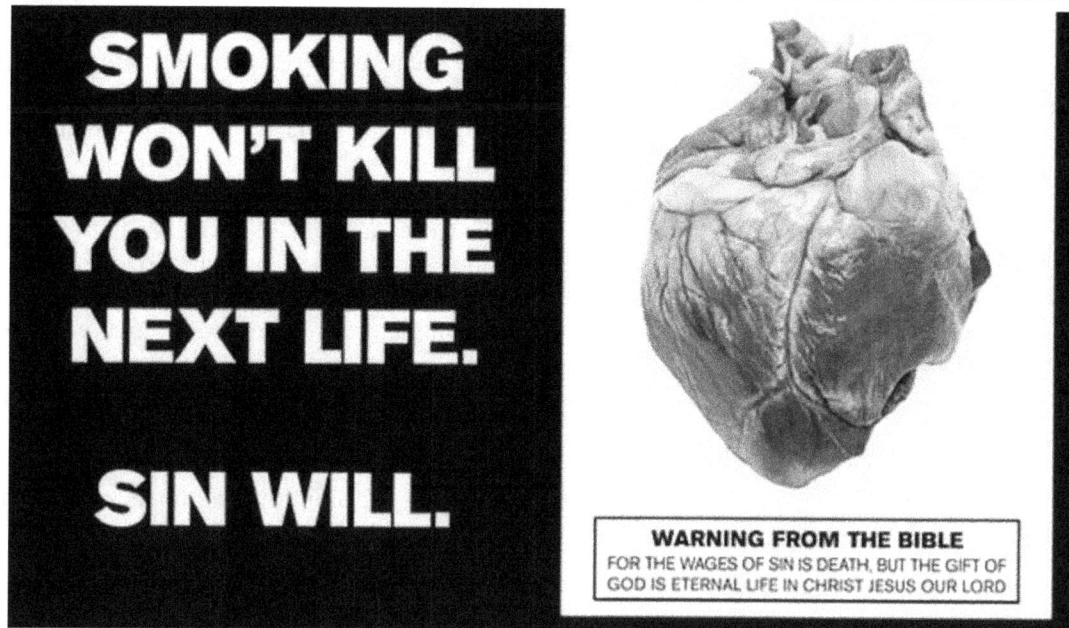

SMOKING WON'T KILL YOU IN THE NEXT LIFE.

SIN WILL.

WARNING FROM THE BIBLE
FOR THE WAGES OF SIN IS DEATH, BUT THE GIFT OF GOD IS ETERNAL LIFE IN CHRIST JESUS OUR LORD

Blessed are the poor, the meek, the pure of heart and clogged of lungs and arteries, for theirs is the kingdom of heaven. After years of being exorcised from every office, restaurant and hotel, smokers have finally found a group accepting them with open arms: the church.

Religious billboards outside many churches in Sydney now preach: "Smoking won't kill you in the next life. Sin will." In a mock-up of graphic health warnings on cigarette packets, the billboard features an image of a bloodied heart and a "warning from the Bible" about spiritual dangers lurking beyond the grave for the sinful.

The light-hearted message, no pun intended, seems to be that smoking is bad but sin is worse. "Better to be a smoker that goes to heaven than a person who doesn't smoke and falls under the judgment of God," the Reverend Andrew Bruce said.

The billboard outside his St Peters Anglican Church, on the Princes Highway, is seen by about 40,000 cars a day, he said. "Jesus is good news for smokers and non-smokers alike." The health risks for smokers are not a patch on the prospect of eternal damnation, he suggested. "One is eternal and one is only for this life; I think that's the point."

But the billboard, produced by Outreach Media, has raised hell with anti-smoking advocates. Anne Jones, chief executive of the Action on Smoking and Health, said it spread the wrong message. "I think it's better to be alive and deal with the religious issues rather than be dead and not be able to deal with anything," she said. "It's trivializing what is a major cause of death and disease and I think it's better to avoid merging the two issues, frankly ... Smoking leaves everything else in the shade."

"I think the biggest sin of the lot is being boring," Bruce said. "If we put up a sign saying 'Jesus loves you,' that's what people expect us to say. You need to strike deeper than that and engage people or it's here today, gone tomorrow."

Amen, brother Bruce.

Anti-tobacco extremist foiled in attempt to bomb snuff factory

Karen Meyers, left, allegedly planned to park a truck full of explosives outside a tobacco factory in order to "protect the children."

OWENSBORO KY- The FBI has finally released details of the sting that resulted in the arrest of 29 year old mother of three Karen Meyers, whom they say planned to blow up the Swedish Match snuff factory outside of Owensboro, Kentucky on October 17th.

Meyers first came to the FBI's attention while in an online political chatroom. Making statements such as "if they elect Romney I'm going to blow up the white house" and "Evereyone [sic] that put Bush in the Oval office should die and I'm all 4 being the 1 to do it", she quickly flew under the Federal Government's radar.

"We have agents who monitor every chatroom on the internet," claimed FBI Director James McJunkin. "The Dragonball Z guy that goes into Pokémon chatrooms just to talk smack? That's one of us. Everyone with an avatar of Barack Obama with his face painted like the Joker, or an avatar of themselves wearing a Guy Fawkes mask? That's us too."

While tracking her movements across the internet, agents became aware of her involvement in several anti-tobacco extremist groups, including Tobacco-Free Kids, TheTruth.com, Action on Smoking and Health (ASH) and KillTheCan.org. "We pulled her voting record and were astonished to see that she voted not only for Obama, but for Henry Waxman as well. We also found a poem entitled "The Lion" that she posted at allpoetry.com in which she mourned the death of Ted Kennedy. It was pretty scary stuff. We decided to close in on her then."

An agent using the screen name "legalizegaymarriage69" approached her and boasted of his "hacktivist" DDoS attacks on several Big Tobacco websites. This apparently impressed her enough to write back to the agent, asking for a pic and complaining that her husband was "just so distant" that it was nice to find another male to chat with who also happened to share her beliefs.

The chat lasted several months, until the agent told the suspect that if she really loved him, she would do something about all the evil smokeless tobacco manufacturers who were marketing snus to schoolchildren. Meyers then posted an ad on Craigslist that stated she was looking for "somebody with a big truck and like, a thousand pound bomb that I could detonate with my iphone 5. I only need it for a few hours and can pay up to 75 bux." Undercover FBI agents instantly responded to the ad and soon arrived at Meyers' door with a rented Krispy Kreme truck that they said was full of explosives. "She said 'oh that is so awesome!' and then asked if one of us could park it in front of the Swedish Match factory. She said that she would pay us an extra five dollars to do so, since she was receiving disability benefits for an injured back and was afraid that she would hurt herself climbing into the truck."

Meyers followed the Krispy Kreme truck in her 2003 Chevy Aveo. The agents told her to dial a certain number on the phone which would then cause the truck to explode. The phone number actually belonged to a local DMV office, which gave the agents ample time to coordinate their apprehension of Mrs. Meyers. "I knew we were looking at about a sixty minute window before the DMV would pick up the phone, but I didn't want to take any chances so we all just jumped out of the bushes at the same time and tazed her repeatedly."

Meyers was brought into custody and sent to Quantico for further questioning to determine whether or not she is part of any other terrorist cells. Suspicions were confirmed when Susan Sarandon offered to pay for Mrs. Meyers legal representation. "The whole thing was pretty kooky," claimed Director McJunkin. "But at least she's off the street, and more importantly, off the internet."

Says WHO

In what has to be the stupidest directive that we at the STE have read this month, the World Health Organization is urging countries to ban E-cig use on the grounds that they **resemble** traditional tobacco cigarettes. The WHO then euthanized this cat, since he resembled Hitler:

Hitler cat: "Say 'nein' to WHO!"

Almost half of England's "Most Wanted" are tobacco smugglers

Eight of the twenty most wanted fugitives in England are wanted in connection to tobacco-smuggling and tax evasion charges. This, compared to six drug dealers, four pedophiles/child sex traffickers, and two murderers, marks a good indication of exactly where Great Britain's legislative priorities lie: strictly up its own arse.

The International Tobacco Growers Association Stages Worldwide Protest to "Unite Farmers, Protect 30 Million Jobs"

LONDON, October 29, 2012 -To mark the first-ever World Tobacco Growers' Day (#WTGD) today, tobacco farmers across the globe are taking part in dozens of events to highlight the disastrous impact World Health Organization proposals will have on their livelihoods if passed by parties to the Framework Convention on Tobacco Control (FCTC) in November.

"We're celebrating the benefits our farms bring to our communities and we're asking our leaders to stand with us, to hear our voices, and to give us the opportunity to work together to protect our way of life," said Antonio Abrunhosa, chief executive officer of the International Tobacco Growers Association (ITGA). Abrunhosa is leading the events worldwide and plans to carry the growers' message to the FCTC's Fifth Conference of the Parties (COP5) in Seoul, Korea next month.

WTGD is the beginning of an annual effort to bring together the world's 30 million tobacco growers. Events in dozens of countries across four continents today demonstrated the social and economic contribution farmers make to their communities and educated the public about the issues impacting their livelihoods.

The 2012 WTGD events focus on the threat currently facing the world's tobacco farmers from the FCTC. "We are also asking governments to join us today and step back from the WHO abyss and protect, not penalize, poor tobacco farmers," Abrunhosa said. He pointed out that these recommendations run contrary to the original intent of the FCTC's treaty, which was to provide "technical and financial assistance to aid the economic transition of tobacco growers and workers" if and when a decline in tobacco consumption results in lower demand for the crop.

"These draconian proposals are putting tobacco farmers under unprecedented attack from bureaucrats who are looking to artificially reduce the supply of tobacco without providing growers any viable alternatives to support their families," said Abrunhosa. "Contrary to FCTC's claims, not a single smoker will stop smoking because of these proposals. All they will do is spread misery among farmers and their families in some of the least developed countries in the world. We are asking the FCTC to respect its own principles and accept growers' knowledge and opinion on issues that impact their livelihoods."

More information about ITGA is available at **www.tobaccoleaf.org**.

Shopping List

All of the new Smokeless Tobacco products that have debuted since last issue

(Note: some products may have been previously released in a different format or re-issued with a new SKU)

- **Thunder White Portions:** Frosted; Wintergreen; Cool Mint; Ultra RAW (v2)

- **Dholakia Christmas Pack**: Blueberry; Plum Cake; Choco Rose (DK)

- **Nordströmmen** Ltd. Edition Moe Unz Jullssnus (v2)

- **Blågul** Original Portion (TC)

- **Poschl Grado** Caffé (Poschl)

- **Kardus 2012** Cincho (SM)

- **Skruf** Organic Selection White Portion; Xtra Strong White Portion (Skruf)

- **Oden's:** all flavors have been reformulated by GN's new master blender Conny Andersson, formerly of Swedish Match North Europe.

- **Granit** Intensive Xtra Strong White; Explosive Xtra Strong Original (F&L)

- **Toque USA:** Black Cherry; Chocolate; Citrus; Espresso; Kentucky Bourbon; Lime; Peach; Rum & Cola; Spanish Brandy; Spearmint; Wild Berry; Whiskey & Honey (Toque/Kretek)

- **Sir Walter Scott's** Fine Border Snuff: Creme de Figue (SJS)

- **Paul Gotard Ltd Edition Collector's Bottles:** Gooseberry, Juniper, Pear & Rhubarb (PG)

- **Bernards Xmas Snuff**: Weinachtpris (BD)

- **Fubar:** Bohica, Doolali Tap, Toasted, Willy Pete (FUBAR)

- **Granit G20** White Portions: Original, Green Mint, Licorice (F&L)

- **Granit G20** Regular Portion Original (F&L)

- **General Mint** (Swedish Edition- not the same blend as the American General Mint) (SMAB)

- **de Kralingse** Molens Windmill Snuff: St. Omer's No. 1 (Molens)

- **Silver Dollar:** Vanilla, Blueberry, Cola, Coffee, Cinnamon, Licorice (Toque)

- **Camel Snuff Pouches**: Dark Milled, Wintergreen (RJR)

- **Skoal Readycut:** Wintergreen, Mint, Straight (USST)

- **Gotlandssnus Julessnus:** Portion and Loose (Limited Edition) (Gotlands)

- **Nordströmmen Julessnus (Limited Christmas Snus):** Loose and Portion (v2)

- **Catch** Strong White Mini Peppermint Portion (SMAB)

- **Art/Dos/White Bite** Dry White Mini Portions (four varieties) (Northerner/TillCe)

- **Viceroy** Snus Pouches: Mint and Natural (RJR

- **Cooper Wintergreen** (re-launch) (Swisher Intl.)

The Road To The White House:
America Elects New Moron To Run The Country

Washington, DC- The nation was stunned recently when *Snuff Taker's Ephemeris* publisher R.W. Hubbard was elected to serve as President of The United States of America.

In what can only be described as a bizarre chain of events, the 30 year old Libertarian candidate from North Carolina was elected in a landslide victory against Mitt Romney (Rep.) and Barack Obama (Dem.).

"I wasn't really trying to run [for office]," claimed Hubbard. "The Electoral College threw a kegger and somehow I ended up on the guest list. I brought several of our new female models with me, along with the Rohypnol that I take for recreational purposes. Let's just say that by the end of the party, everyone was feeling pretty good."

The Electoral College is the legislative body that chooses the President in every election. "For some stupid reason, citizens still vote for the President every four years, as if their vote mattered," claimed College Elector Glen Dunlap. "We're the ones who actually decide who holds office. Winning the Popular Vote is like winning a toaster oven in a church raffle. You've got to come through us, and you better bring your 'A' game."

This puts the surprise victory into a better perspective. "Last time, Barry won us over with his *killer*-ass bud that he flew in from Hawaii. But McCain also showed up with Sarah Palin, who is well-known for her ability to perform certain sex acts with several men at the same time. It was a tough decision to say the least."

Not so this time, added fellow Elector Anni Chung. "Obama shows up empty handed, saying he just needed a little more time to be re-elected and he would be able to score some weed. And Romney shows up wearing a sweater vest and carrying a twelve pack of Tab. But then here comes Rob with the roofies and the chicks, looking all like a rock star. There was no competition at all," she said. Chung also noted that she liked his eyes.

President Hubbard seemed almost as surprised as the rest of the world when he was named Commander-in-Chief. "We all woke up about noon, and everyone was shaking my hand, saying I was going to do a fine job. I didn't know what the hell they were talking about."

(**LEFT TO RIGHT**): VICE PRESIDENT MICK CHENEY, PRESIDENT-ELECT ROBERT HUSSEIN HUBBARD, AND SECRETARY OF STATE MICAH RODHAM RIMEL-AL ABID.

(LEFT): VP Mick issues new directive from the Oval Office. The document consisted entirely of misspelled swear words and crudely-rendered stick figures farting on each other.

(Right): Secretary of State Micah, imploring America to "turn away from your false gods and say you love satan." His rousing speech was met with massive applause from the audience.

Hubbard was quickly sworn in on a stack of STE's. "You da president now, yo," shouted Howard Lamb of Nebraska. Hubbard was then shuttled out to the White House to give his commencement speech, which was accompanied to the strains of Pigmeat Markham's *Here Comes The Judge.*

"I'm not going to make any promises this day," he began. "Because like every president before me, I'll just break them all one by one. But I can guarantee this. Every time you see my lips moving, you can rest assured that I am lying. I'm lying to you, the American people, and I'm lying to the rest of the world as well." This statement was well received by the attendees, who cheered and fist-pumped for several minutes.

"The first thing I'm going to do is legalize drugs, prostitution and partial-birth tobacco harvesting. Second, I'll make it mandatory for all non-criminals to own a gun, that way crime will be kept to an absolute minimum. Then I'll pull all of our troops out of foreign countries, dismantle the standing army, and put them all to work in US factories building things that we formerly bought from China."

"Furthermore, I've dismantled the Electoral College, fired our representatives in both Houses, and instilled a system of direct democracy by which each citizen votes on every issue directly via Facebook or Twitter. The only caveat is that you have to pass a minimum IQ test in order to vote, since most of you are too stupid to understand how our system functions."

At the ceremony, attendees openly wept tears of joy and raised their hands skyward, as if they were thanking God for electing Hubbard. "Obama promised me a Cadillac," said Mrs. Bertice Johnson of Oxford, Mississippi. "Here it is four years later and I still got a Buick. Mr. Hubbard says that not only will I get the Cadillac, I'll get *two* Cadillacs. He truly is a great man."

The President then announced his "Snus Initiative," which would put the Swedish tobacco product into the homes of every American family, free of charge. The Norwegian Nobel Committee reported that they were "moving as fast as humanly possible" to finish the engravings on Hubbard's forthcoming Nobel Peace Prize.

"With snus in the mouths of every American, no one will ever want to fight again. We're also giving him the Nobel Prize for Medicine, since 99% of all tobacco-related deaths will disappear overnight when they give up cigarettes for smokeless." (Hubbard was previously awarded the Nobel Prize for Literature two years ago for his work in *The Snuff Taker's Ephemeris.*)

After the speech, Hubbard, Hellwig and Rimel entered the White House in slow motion, without looking behind them. Later in the day, Former President Obama returned to the White House to gather his belongings, which had been shoved into black plastic garbage bags and tossed unceremoniously onto the south lawn. Several observers reported seeing Secretary of State Rimel and Press Secretary Conny Andersson urinating on Obama's limousine. "I know it's wrong," shouted Andersson. "But at the same time it feels so right!"

STE

High Hopes

November 7th- Washington and Colorado voters have approved the legalization of marijuana for recreational use. Adult growers, distributors and users of marijuana are now free to engage in a practice that in some states could net them life in prison. Let's hope that this will lead to an increase in tobacco-rights activists groups who will similarly champion the decriminalization of other "soft" drugs, such as smokeless tobacco. (Washington and Colorado have some of the strictest tobacco laws and taxes in the nation.)

Massachusetts passed a similar ballot initiative the same day, legalizing medical marijuana use. Paradoxically, George N. Peterson (assistant minority leader for the Commonwealth of Massachusettes) introduced Bill H.1512, which would "prohibit the distribution, possession and use of all tobacco products."

In what was initially thought to be an internet hoax or the work of clever hackers, the *Ephemeris* contacted Mr. Peterson's office for comment. Speaking off the record, a staff employee sheepishly admitted that the Bill was in fact not a hoax and was something that "we hope will find the right sponsors in the weeks forthcoming." The spokesperson sounded really ashamed and embarrassed while having to answer questions about the Bill and we hope that he or she is able to find future employment with a politician who is not suffering from dementia.

Snuff Sales up 34% in Iceland

As cigarettes become more expensive in Iceland, people are turning to cheaper alternatives like RYO and smokeless.

Although moist snuff/snus is banned in Iceland, popular brands of snuff like Neftobak are marketed as nasal snuff but are most often used orally, sometimes with snuffer adding extra water to the container in order to make it aesthetically closer to Swedish-style snus.

Though the health benefits of switching to smokeless are not allowed to be promoted by tobacco companies (just like in the USA), some companies have begun to advertise that switching from cigarettes to snuff will save you up to 70% each year.

Graphic Cigarette Warning Pack Decision up for Appeal

The FDA's proposed cigarette pack warning photos mandate, backed by President Obama, is struggling to remain alive in the US judicial system. The law would force all cigarette companies to put large warning labels on the front of the pack backed by disgusting pictures like diseased lungs, tracheotomy holes, underdeveloped fetuses, and other family-friendly moneyshots.

The Justice Department filed a petition October 8th asking for the Appellate courts to rehear the case after the U.S. Court of Appeals in Washington affirmed lower court's ruling blocking the mandate, saying it ran afoul of the First Amendment's free speech protections. The court rarely grants such appeals.

In a 2-1 decision, the appeals court panel wrote that the case raises "novel questions about the scope of the government's authority to force the manufacturer of a product to go beyond making purely factual and accurate commercial disclosures and undermine its own economic interest; in this case, by making "every single pack of cigarettes in the country [a] mini billboard' for the government's anti-smoking message."

According to the Appellate court, the FDA "has not provided a shred of evidence" showing that the warnings will "directly advance" the number of Americans who smoke. But in its appeal seeking a full court rehearing, the government argued that the text of the new warnings are "indisputably accurate" and the format, including the use of graphics, is tailored to the demand of a "market in which the vast majority of users become addicted to a lethal product before age 18."

Hey, FDA, why not enforce existing tobacco laws instead of making new ones? Oh, right, that would require logical action on your part, which we know that your agency is incapable of. Go eat some Chantix.

Crooked Politician Alert: John Dalli resigns as EU Commissioner After Trying to Extort Swedish Match

As we were going to press, news broke concerning the scandal in the EU. John Dalli, head of the committee reviewing the European import ban on snus, was implicated in a complicated extortion plot that has yet to be fully disclosed. It seems that Mr. Dalli sent a business associate over to Swedish Match in an attempt to extort money from them, with the promise that Dalli would in turn act in favor of the snus company in future EU proceedings. Below is the entire transcript released by the EU in response to the situation. We guarantee that we will be following this story closely and will print further updates as they come along.

EU PRESS RELEASE: BRUSSELS, OCTOBER 16 2012- Commissioner John Dalli has today announced his resignation as a member of the Commission, with immediate effect.

Mr Dalli informed the President of the European Commission Jose Manuel Barroso of his decision following an investigation by OLAF, the EU's antifraud office, into a complaint made in May 2012 by the tobacco producer, Swedish Match. The company alleged that a Maltese entrepreneur had used his contacts with Mr Dalli to try to gain financial advantages from the company in return for seeking to influence a possible future legislative proposal on tobacco products, in particular on the EU export ban on snus. As soon as the Commission received the complaint it immediately requested OLAF to investigate.

The OLAF final report was sent to the Commission on 15 October. It found that the Maltese entrepreneur had approached the company using his contacts with Mr Dalli and sought to gain financial advantages in exchange for influence over a possible future legislative proposal on snus. No transaction was concluded between the company and the entrepreneur and no payment was made. The OLAF report did not find any conclusive evidence of the direct participation of Mr Dalli but did consider that he was aware of these events.

The OLAF report showed clearly that the European Commission's decision making process and the position of the services concerned has not been affected at all by the matters under investigation.

The final OLAF report and its recommendations are being sent by OLAF to the Attorney General of Malta. It will now be for the Maltese judiciary to decide how to follow up.

After the President informed Mr Dalli about the report received from OLAF, Mr Dalli decided to resign in order to be able to defend his reputation and that of the Commission. Mr Dalli categorically rejects these findings.

Mr Barroso has decided that Vice President Maros Sefcovic will take over the portfolio of Mr Dalli on an interim basis until a new Commissioner of Maltese nationality is appointed in accordance with article 246 (2) of the Treaty on the functioning of the European Union.

ElishaC Photography

Bygone Brands

Special Edition by
Bill Johnson

Publisher's note: *Every time I talk to Bill I whine about a certain snuff or snus brand being pulled off the market. I was telling him how Swedish Match dropped General Green Harvest from their catalog and Bill reeled off a list of all the brands of tobacco that he used to buy that weren't manufactured anymore. I told him to write an article about it sometime and he ignored me. That is, until he went into the store to buy a box of Muriel Air Tip Cigars and found out that they were no longer being sold. Then he got mad. (I had known about the discontinuation of Air Tips for about six months but didn't have the heart to break the news to Bill. He and I both loved the little cheapo cigars, but I haven't been smoking them for 30 years like Bill has.) "Dammit," Bill said, "I guess I'm going to write about all those brands that I used to use that they quit making." Here's how it turned out.*

Tobacco Products That I Used To Use Before Some Idiot Decided To Quit Making Them

1. Cigarettes: I've been a Chesterfield King smoker for years simply because when they quit making a brand I like, I fall back Chesterfields. They've never gone away, so I'm pretty loyal to them even though I'm not too crazy about the flavor.

I guess the first cigarette I smoked that I actually liked was Old Gold. When I was a kid, it was either Old Gold or Fatima's for me. Then I found a brand called Picayune, which was one of the best cigarettes ever made. About the time I went into the service, they quit manufacturing the above three brands, so I picked up Chesterfields for a few years.

When I got out of the service, I started smoking Raleigh cigarettes, which were really good for the time. When they stopped manufacturing the filterless version, I started on Phillip Morris Commanders, which were decent. Eventually the Commanders were discontinued, so I was back to the drawing board.

This was during the late sixties and early seventies, and I figured I'd try my hand at the new gimmicky filtered cigarettes. From my days spent working with RJ Reynolds, I stayed away from Camel and Winstons because of their high percentage of recon tobacco. Recon tobacco is basically floor sweepings that are pressed into a sheet and sliced up into new tobacco shreds. They spray the crap out of it with casings and God knows what else in order to give it flavor. This was the period in which cigarettes stopped tasting unique and all began tasting kind of uniformly dull. (Coincidentally, this was the peak of popularity for pipe smoking in the United States, which I always thought had to do with the fact that cigarette smokers that had been smoking since before about 1960 were used to actually tasting the tobacco in their cigarettes. I have no idea why kids pick up the habit today. There's no flavor and they all smell like burning cardboard. But I think many cigarette smokers switched to the pipe because the tobacco made for pipes at that time beat the pants off of anything that came twenty to a pack. Plus it was cheaper, and women loved the aroma of most brands.)

Speaking of pipe tobacco and cigarettes, a "new" brand came along in the mid sixties that I smoked for almost the entire time they were available: Half and Half brand pipe tobacco cigarettes. It wasn't quite the same blend as Half and Half pipe tobacco, but it was close. It definitely had a nice aroma and fuller flavor than the Lucky Strike filters did. But the joy was shortlived; after a couple of years H&H was gone and I was back to Chesterfields. But one thing that Half and Half cigarettes introduced me to was the 100mm length filtered cigarette, which I cottoned to pretty quickly. Possibly the one advantage that I see for filtered cigarettes over non-filters is that you can actually smoke the entire cigarette if it's filtered. To do that with a Chesterfield you would need a cigarette holder.

Great new taste: pipe tobacco in a filter cigarette!

PIPE TOBACCO IN A FILTER CIGARETTE

A CARGO OF CONTENTMENT IN A FILTER CIGARETTE

HALF AND HALF

You get pleasing aroma—and a great new taste! The secret? This filter cigarette is packed with America's best-tasting pipe tobacco—famous Half and Half! Smoke new Half and Half Filter Cigarettes. There's a cargo of contentment in store for you!

Product of The American Tobacco Company

Half and Half cigarettes. According to Bill Johnson, a good brand that may have been ahead of its time:

"A few years later, Middleton came out with their Cherry Blend Cigar, and all of the sudden there was a flood of tipped cigars comprised of pipe tobacco.

But as far as I know, Half and Half cigarettes were the first [brand] to combine the idea of putting aromatic pipe tobacco into a more convenient, smokable form. I doubt we would have Black and Milds today if it weren't for Half and Half."

Get in on thin.

Silva Thins—
lowest in 'tar' and nicotine*
of all 100's,
lower than most Kings.
Yet better taste.

Silva Thin
The one that's in

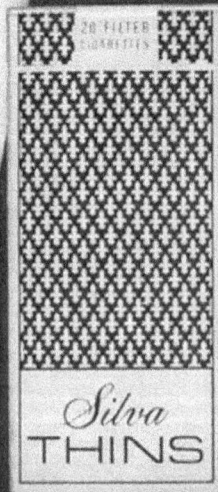

Regular

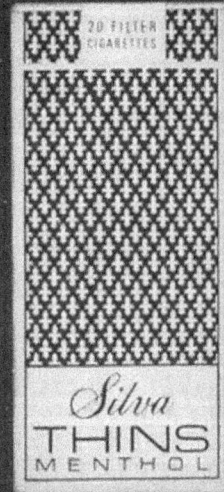

Menthol

*According to latest U.S. Government figures

I think the reason Half and Half ultimately failed was that while it could ultimately be smoked like a cigarette, the PH was the same as the pipe tobacco, which meant that the smoker was inhaling a lot of tobacco but not getting a fix on the nicotine. (A line of Prince Albert cigarettes came out at the same time and was engineered the same way.) If you smoked it like a pipe, you would ultimately receive satisfaction, but only after about five cigarettes back to back (if they were the King size) or after two or three (if they were 100s.) They were too much a cigarette for pipe smokers and too much pipe tobacco for cigarette smokers. But for the guys like me that smoked both, they were tops.

On into the seventies, I smoked Silva Thins for several years. Silva Thins were unique in that they were a low tar cigarette that actually had flavor for miles. They were closer to a Marlboro Red than a Marlboro Light in nicotine hit, and they had a really long filter that meant I could carry it around in my lip like I do my pipe and not have any smoke get in my eyes.

Silva Thins died out and I soon switched to the first premium "luxury" cigarette on the market: Benson and Hedges. During the 70's, B&H cost almost twice as much as regular brands, but the tobacco that was in it was top notch, with very little recon added to it. But during the Reagan Era the manufacturing process was changed and Benson and Hedges became "just another brand", with a slightly lower price and a lot more recon.

So I went back to Chesterfields, and I've been with them pretty much steady for the last 30 years. I only smoke about three cigarettes a day, so it's not like I'm so discerning in taste that I have to special order English Ovals or Craven A in order to reach satisfaction. I did change for a while to Harley Davidson cigarettes in the 1990s, because they were dirt cheap and tasted like Chesterfields. But then they screwed all that up by adding a bunch more recon and renaming the brand "Mavericks", which are still around. But a lot of people would be surprised to find out they started out as Harley Davidsons.

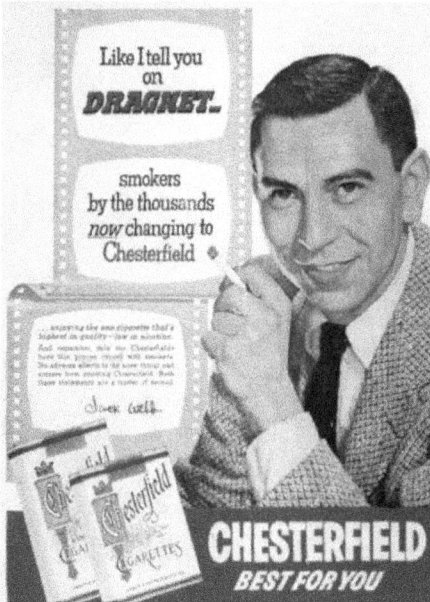

Clockwise from top: "Bill Brands."
1. A carton of Harley Davidsons.

2. Benson & Hedges: 'You pay more... You get more.'

3. Between Fatima, Chesterfields and Camel, Jack Webb endorsed his fair share of cigarette brands before succumbing to lung cancer.

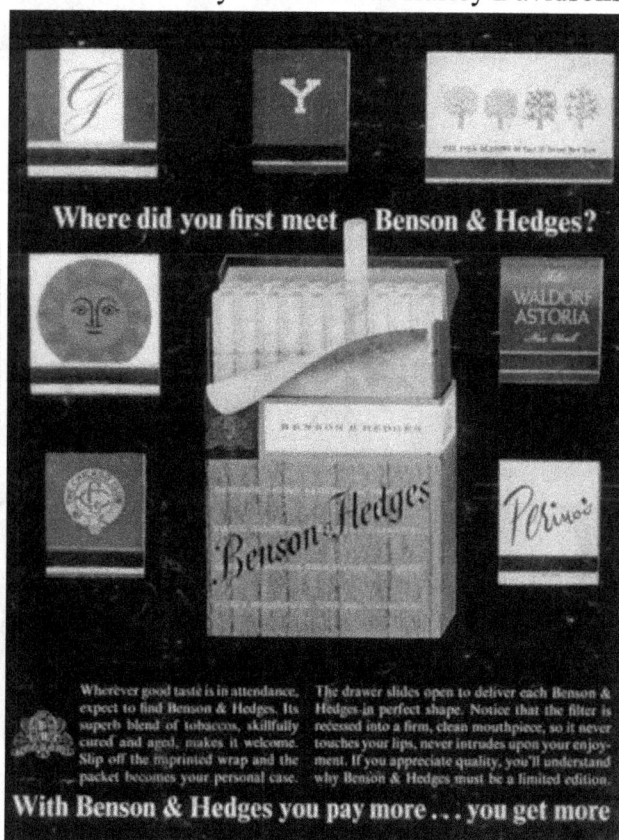

Where did you first meet Benson & Hedges?

With Benson & Hedges you pay more ... you get more

Introducing an old way to enjoy tobacco.

If you're one of the millions who like to smoke, chances are you think that smoking is the only way to really enjoy tobacco.

Well, we have news for you:

There's more than one way to enjoy the pleasures of the tobacco leaf.

As a matter of fact, people have been partaking of these pleasures in ways that have nothing to do with smoking for hundreds of years.

Satisfying the aristocrats:

Take the aristocracy in England.

As far back as the 16th century, they considered it a mark of distinction — as well as a source of great satisfaction — to use finely-cut, finely-ground tobacco with the quaint-sounding name of "snuff". At first, this "snuff" was, as the name suggests, inhaled through the nose.

Just a pinch:

Later on, the vogue of sniffing gave way to an even more pleasurable form of using tobacco — placing just a pinch in the mouth between cheek and gum and letting it rest there.

Now, hundreds of years later, this form of tobacco is having the biggest growth in popularity since the days of Napoleon.

And what we call "smokeless tobacco" is becoming a favorite way of enjoying tobacco with Americans from all walks of life.

Anything but obvious:

Why is "smokeless tobacco" becoming so popular in America?

There are a number of reasons.

One of the obvious ones is that it is a way of enjoying tobacco that is anything but obvious.

In other words, you can enjoy it any of the times or places where smoking is not permitted.

Thus, lawyers and judges who cannot smoke in the courtroom, scientists who cannot smoke in the laboratory, and many people who like to smoke on the job, but aren't allowed to, often become enthusiastic users.

In the same way, people who work or play with their hands get the comfort of tobacco — but don't have to strike a match or worry about how to hold (or where to put) their cigarette, cigar, or pipe.

The big four:

The four best-known, best-liked brands of "smokeless tobacco" are "Copenhagen", "Skoal" and the two flavors of "Happy Days".

All four are made by the United States Tobacco Company, but each has a distinctive flavor and personality. (To make sure that distinctive flavor is as fresh as it should be when you buy it, all cans are dated on the bottom.)

Copenhagen, the biggest-selling brand in the world, has the rich flavor of pure tobacco. Skoal is wintergreen-flavored. And Happy Days comes in either raspberry or mint flavor — so it's especially popular with beginners.

But if "smokeless tobacco" has many advantages for lovers of tobacco, we must also admit it has one disadvantage.

How to use it:

It takes a little more time and practice to learn exactly how much to use (a "tiny pinch" is the best way to describe it) and exactly how to use it.

To get over that minor problem, we'll be happy to send you a free booklet that explains how to get the full enjoyment of "smokeless tobacco" — as well as a few pinches that you can try for yourself.

(Write to "Smokeless Tobacco", United States Tobacco Company, Dept. P11, Greenwich, Connecticut 06830.)

Once you get the knack, you'll find you have something else, too: Another great way to enjoy tobacco.

Smokeless Tobacco. A pinch is all it takes.

2. Moist Snuff.

If you'll have read my column in the first edition of this magazine, you'll remember that I didn't try my first can of moist snuff until the Korean war. At that time, the only real "national" brand that I knew of was Copenhagen, which was decent, but not a flavor that I really cared for.

There was a brand called Viking Snuff which tasted damned close to Grov Snus from what I remember. The packaging was all blue with a little Viking ship on it. I picked up a can wherever I could find it, which wasn't very often and after the late 60's it just seemed to disappear.

When I was in the mood for a mint or wintergreen flavored snuff, I didn't run to Skoal. I preferred Work Mate. I have no idea when this left the market but it seems like it was in production into the seventies. The cans kept much fresher than Skoal did at the time, which was good for a guy like me that took about a week to kill a can of minty snuff.

Probably the best dip that ever came out was Hawken. Not this green Hawken that they sell now, but the original "straight" Hawken. Man, this stuff was good. It was wet, it packed well, and it was a crazy cut; a mixture of extra long thin strands, small chunks like chewing tobacco, and extra fine granules like Swedish snus. Rumor had it that Hawken was made up of all the different remainders of other brands that were left in the line, but I doubt it. There was a sweetness in the background of Hawken that was unique to all other moist snuff brands before or since. I have no idea why they stopped manufacturing it.

Around this time, USST manufactured three brands that vendors dubbed "the big three": Copenhagen, Skoal and Key. I was never a fan of Key but knew a lot of guys out west that used it. It was pretty much a Copenhagen clone from what I could tell, but it was sold at a budget price so it must have been a lower grade of tobacco.

During the late 70's, USST replaced Key with Happy Days, which was a raspberry flavored dip. Later on they tried Apple, Cherry and Mint, among others. The Apple and Raspberry were the best of the lot, and I used them quite a bit during the eighties. USST later dropped the Happy Days line but brought some of the flavors back under the Skoal label. Apple was there, but Raspberry was gone for good. (The "Skoal Key" of recent years is supposedly the same recipe as the original Key, but it's not, according to my memory.)

I'm sad to see that all of the pouched Skoal flavors have been replaced with "Rich" and "Crisp" or whatever they're called now. The flavored pouches were a good way to introduce a smoker to safer smokeless products. I used to recommend the Vanilla and Apple, which we still have in granulated form, but pouches are more appealing to first time users in my experience. I got a guy to give up a 40 year cigarette habit with Skoal Berry Pouches. I've also tried the Skoal Snus, and it tastes a lot like the old Workmate brand. I think I'll stick with the Swedish stuff, thank you.

I tried a can of the elusive Dark Milled Camel Snuff, and I was sorry to see that it never went into a wider production. It was every bit as good as any of the other brands out there. I say that if there's still room in the market for crap like Silver Creek and Gold River, then bring back Camel Snuff. The tin was a top notch design in my book.

Left, *Trademark Registration for* Hawken Straight, *manufactured from 1980-1982.*

Right: Workmate Mint *and* Viking Snuff. *Aside from products bearing variations of the "Seal" name* **(Below, Left)** *, "Viking" is perhaps the most overused brand name in smokeless tobacco history.*

Workmate *was originally also available in a natural flavor* **(Right)** *but it was quickly overshadowed by the succcess of the Mint, which was* Skoal's *biggest competitor for many years.*

(Below, L-R): *Pair of print ads for* Camel Snuff *and* Skoal Pouches.

3. Dry Snuffs.

I've been extremely fortunate in that almost all of the big brands that I grew up with are still around today. Except for DeVoe. I've heard that the last one they were making, Eagle Mills Scotch, is gone now too, but unless you were around back in the forties you might not know that there was an entire line of DeVoe products besides the Eagle Mills, mainly Sweet, German and Salted. It was a good brand that I think deserves to be here today every bit as much as Railroad Mills or Society.

[**Editor's note:** *I'd like to pass on a bit of trivia that Bill recently shared with me regarding Society snuff. Bill says that way back when, Society was only used by women and was considered a feminine snuff, sort of a dry snuff version of Virginia Slims or Capri cigarettes. To see a man using Society back then would have been like seeing a man wearing a dress.*]

Back in the early 70's, there was a brand called Coke that I only ever saw at 7-11 convenience stores. When they shut down all of the 7-11s in North Carolina (about 1975) I never saw it again. It came in a few flavors and had a sort of coarse, moist texture like a Rappee.

Cherry Cokesnuff. Made in England, sold through 7-11 stores around 1971-75. If anyone knows which company blended this brand, please let us know.

The Makers of KING EDWARD CIGARS Offer..

20 FREE TRIPS to Sunny FLORIDA
To The Ten Grand Prize Winners

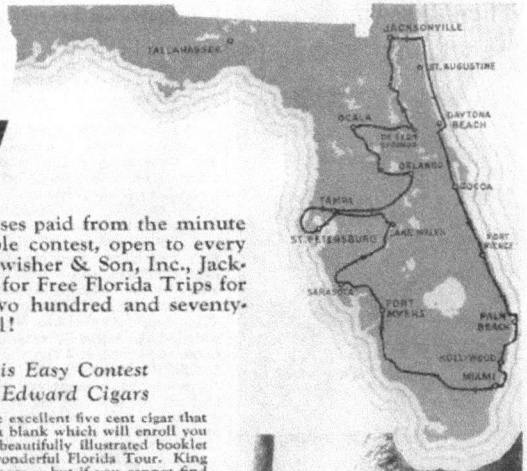

All Expenses Paid
10 Days of Fun!

A WINTER VACATION—under summer skies! And all expenses paid from the minute you leave your home until you return. Here's an easy, simple contest, open to every resident of Continental United States, except employees of Jno. H. Swisher & Son, Inc., Jacksonville, Fla., and its advertising agency. Ten Grand Prizes—calling for Free Florida Trips for twenty people. Twenty-five Cash Prizes—totalling $1000. And two hundred and seventy-five merchandise prizes—making three hundred and ten prizes in all!

Free Booklet Describes Complete Itinerary

Listed below are the beautiful modern hotels where guests will be entertained during their sojourn in Florida.

HOTEL GEORGE WASHINGTON
Jacksonville
SEASIDE INN, *Daytona Beach*
HOTEL EL VERANO
West Palm Beach
ALCAZAR HOTEL, *Miami*
MIRAMAR HOTEL, *Sarasota*
HOTEL THOMAS JEFFERSON
Tampa
SAN JUAN HOTEL, *Orlando*
PONCE DE LEON SPRINGS
HOTEL, *De Leon Springs*

Florida Tour—Personally Conducted by Colonial Stages

JACKSONVILLE and Jacksonville Beach—Ocean Drive to historic St. Augustine—Ocean Drive to Ormond Beach and Daytona Beach. Then through the beautiful Indian River orange country to Palm Beach and West Palm Beach. Coastal Highway through many interesting cities and towns, such as Boca Raton, Ft. Lauderdale, Hollywood-by-the-Sea, Miami, Miami Beach, Coral Gables, Indian Village. Then across the Everglades by way of the famous Tamiami Trail, through Naples, Ft. Myers, to Sarasota. Next, the beautiful inland lake country—Lake Annie, Lake Wales, the Bok Tower, Then Tampa, St. Petersburg, Clearwater, Orlando, Ocala, the famous Silver Springs, beautiful De Leon Springs and the St. Johns River route back to Jacksonville.

Ten days in sunny Florida—all expenses paid. See your King Edward dealer at once. Contest closes Thanksgiving Day.

Secure Entry Blank for This Easy Contest from Any Dealer in King Edward Cigars

Call at any store that sells King Edward — the excellent five cent cigar that is made in Florida. The dealer will give you a blank which will enroll you in this contest and which will bring you a beautifully illustrated booklet giving complete information regarding this wonderful Florida Tour. King Edward Cigars are on sale practically everywhere — but if you cannot find a King Edward dealer in your locality, write direct to us and we will send you entry blank, booklet describing the trip and complete information.

Contest Closes Thanksgiving Day, Nov. 26, 1931. Florida Tour Starts January 11, 1932

Ten Grand Prizes. One all-expense trip for each winner and any companion he chooses. Twenty Free Trips in all. And three hundred other valuable cash and merchandise prizes.

Four simple questions to answer in a letter containing not to exceed 250 words. In case of tie, duplicate prizes will be awarded. Contest winners will be notified as soon after Thanksgiving Day as possible. The Judges will be Jno. T. Alsop, Jr., Mayor of Jacksonville, Fla., Robert Kloeppel, Owner-Director of George Washington Hotel, Jacksonville, Fla., and C. L. Jaycox, Vice-Pres., The Mumm-Romer-Jaycox Advertising Agency, Columbus, Ohio.

Four Easy Questions. Nothing to Buy. Enroll at Once.

Just a little effort and you may win a wonderful trip to Florida. Think of the warm sunshine, the blue skies, the wide sand beaches, the breaking surf, the palm trees, the orange groves, the beautiful hotels and the historic scenes of this great tropical playground — and decide *now* to enter this interesting contest. No coupons to clip. No bands to save. Simply ask any King Edward Cigar dealer for contest entry blank—or, if there is no King Edward dealer in your locality, write direct to

KING EDWARD CIGARS
Jacksonville, Fla.

KING EDWARD 5c

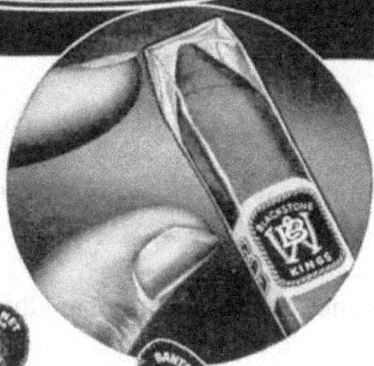

Recently, one of the boys from the magazine sent me some Spanish Jewel, which I understand is worth its weight in gold and will never be made again. A shame, as it's a fine snuff. The Toque version [*Spanish Gem*] hasn't got a scratch on it.

Other than that, I've been pretty fortunate in that I can still go down to the store and pick up a can of Honeybee just like I could when I was five years old. The same can be said for most of the pipe tobacco I enjoy, too, except the Half & Half they sell now isn't the Half & Half *I* used for fifty years. (If you can find an older can that doesn't say "improved cut," you've found the Real McCoy.)

4. Cigars. Tragically, I've outlived all of my favorite cigar brands. That's actually what prompted me to write this article in the first place. Your publisher informed me that Altadis has killed off my Muriel Pipe Aroma Air Tips, the best machine made cigar of all time. [**Publisher's note:** *Unfortunately Bill is correct, and it happened right after he got me hooked on the damn things.*] I've been smoking a pack a week of Air Tips since 1982, and I go down to Food Lion the other day and guess what's missing from the shelf? After I found out that they were discontinued, I felt as though I'd lost my best friend.

I'm digging around for a suitable replacement. Aromatic Tiparillos are the closest I've found so far, but they burn way too quickly. Anyone has any suggestions, drop me a line care of the magazine.

I guess the first cigar brand I remember losing was a King Edward Panetela. This was before they made the Imperials or had the five-pack "pocket humidor." King Edward was a very popular brand back in the 30's and made several shapes and sizes, and you could only buy them singly or by the 50-count box. For some reason the Imperial size became really popular during the war and they phased out all of the other shapes, including the Panetelas I had been smoking since I was first old enough to steal them from my dad's dresser.

Swisher has resurrected the Blackstone name for cheap pipe tobacco cigars now, but when I was a kid, Blackstone was a premium brand that cost almost a nickel more than a King Edward, which was a significant amount for a cigar back then. When the trend went towards bigger cigars, Blackstone dropped their regular size in favor of a Churchill that I didn't care for. (I've always preferred slim cigars; the wider ring gauge just feels clumsy in my mouth).

From there I moved on to Golden's Blue Ribbon Cigars. I would alternate them with Roi-Tan and Hav-a-Tampas, but the Cuban embargo killed the flavor in most American cigars of that era, with the exception of El Producto, which was still pretty flavorful. I smoked them up until 1982 when they went to a homogenized wrapper and I switched to Muriels.

Ehh, all good things must come to an end though. Notice I didn't mention anything about handmade cigars. They all taste about the same to me. I bet that if you were to take 75% of all premium cigar smokers and blindfold them, they wouldn't be able to tell the difference between a Munniemaker or a Montecristo, or a Marsh-Wheeling from a Macanudo. Just ask Mark Twain, Arthur Conan Doyle or George Burns- when you pay a lot for a certain brand, you're pretty much paying for a fancy wrapper band. Save the hassle and go for the cigar with no band and pray it isn't rolled too tight. Or, just bypass all of that nonsense and buy a machine made cigar; they're practically guaranteed to burn evenly. Don't pay attention to what others say about your thriftiness: God blessed us with two middle fingers specifically for this purpose.

STE

GENUINE

R. A. PATTERSON TOBACCO CO.

LUCKY STRIKE

RICH'D, VA.

ROLL CUT

PREPARED FOR THE PIPE

Whenever You See a Pipe You'll Think of LUCKY STRIKE

10c
At All
Dealers

16-oz.
package
90c

160 Years of Lucky Strike

1852: A young doctor out of Henrico County, Virginia comes across a patch of black land dirt on his father-in-law's property. Newlywed Doctor Richard Archibald Patterson has been struggling for a year to get his medical practice off the ground. Most days are spent walking around aimlessly on the four acres he inherited from his wife's father, praying for patients to come in and start his cash flow. Deeply in debt from medical school, he was desperate for business, even taking on the odd veterinary work mending horses.

No one knows exactly what prompted him to plant that first patch of burley in the barren black soil behind his home. Maybe he had some extra seeds that he threw down, not expecting anything to grow. Maybe he was trying to determine just how infertile his land was.

But within a couple of weeks, the leaves had sprouted. Big, pretty coronas were blooming faster than he could top them. The neighbors were mystified, as tobacco wasn't particularly native to that area of Henrico County. "Probably won't be no good after curing," some of the neighbors scoffed. "All show, no cash."

But after the plants had matured and were thrown into the barn, an unusually bright gold-colored strain of burley, teaming with sweetness, cured quickly and tasted great naturally. There was no need to case it in molasses or any of the other common flavorings of the day- it was edible right out of the barn.

Patterson's father-in-law was impressed. "You figgerd I gave you a dust bowl, but here you went and hit a lucky strike!" The second crop was even better, and the third surpassed the first two. Soon RA Patterson was roping up his plug and selling it throughout the county. People came from miles around to buy Doc Patterson's Lucky Strike chew. By 1856 he was packaging it and selling it to stores all over Virginia.

When the Civil War broke out, Patterson enlisted as a surgeon in the 56th Virginia Regiment. He always carried a couple of pounds of his tobacco with him to pass on to seriously wounded men, to help comfort them in some small fashion as they underwent excruciating battlefield amputations. For many a dying Confederate, the last thing they ever tasted was Lucky Strike plug.

After the war, Patterson founded the R.A. Patterson Tobacco Company, as the fame of his Lucky Strike brand had spread throughout the south during the Civil War. In 1871, he introduced a new version of Lucky Strike, this time in a sliced cut plug format which made it easier to be smoked in a pipe or cigarette. The new Lucky proved to be so successful that it was distributed outside of Patterson's native Virginia for the very first time. The sliced plug was later phased out in favor of a roll cut, pretty close in texture to modern RYO tobacco.

By 1903, Patterson had tired of the tobacco business, and his company changed hands to a couple of smaller companies before being finally bought out by Buck Duke's American Tobacco Company in 1905. Dr. Patterson, after retiring from the tobacco industry, involved himself in local politics and still continued to see patients in his private practice. Patterson died peacefully in his sleep on April 8th, 1912, aged 86. He was buried in the Hollywood Cemetery in Richmond Virginia.

1915 brought the first pre-rolled Lucky Strike cigarette, designed to compete head to head with the enormously popular Camel brand. By the 1930's, Lucky Strike had become the best selling cigarette in America, a position that gradually dwindled to a tiny percentage of the market by the 1990's. Still manufactured in its original non-filter form (USA), filtered versions (Europe), RYO pouch (Germany) and Snus (Sweden, Norway), the Lucky brand seems poised for a revival any day now.

Little would R.A. Patterson know that within a few short years of his death, the tobacco he planted in a patch of black dirt would reach worldwide acclaim and still be manufactured today, 160 years after that first sprout.

Chronology of Lucky Strike Packaging

The preceding article in this month's SBT column inspired us to dig up a menagerie of historic Lucky Strike packaging. You can almost chart the trends in tobacco use by the containers that Lucky Strike used. In 1871, cut plug tobacco reigned as king of pre-packaged tobacco. Plugs could be chewed or smoked in a pipe, or ground into snuff, and rolled into cigarettes

1856

1856-1870: The R.A. Patterson company introduces Lucky Strike plug tobacco in a wax paper box with the tagline "Good for a chew, smoking too!" A regional hit with the miners of Virginia, it later becomes available in an easier-to-manage cut plug.

1860s: Patterson introduces Lucky Strike Cut Plug tobacco in a felt bag with metal tag, common for tobacco of that era.

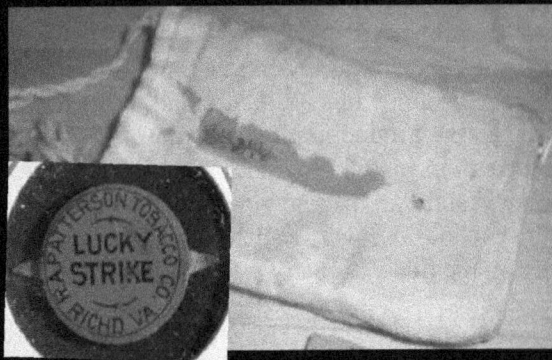

1871: Lucky Strike Sliced Plug now available in metal containers, ranging from lidded tins to round canisters.

1900-1910: With chewing tobacco on its way out and smoking tobacco on its way in, Lucky Strike gradually phases in a "roll cut" (finer cut, like modern pipe tobacco). The label eventually adds "PREPARED FOR THE PIPE" description.

1911-1914: The "Roll Cut" goes nationwide (it was previously available only in Virginia) and the description on the tin eventually changes to "FOR PIPE OR CIGARETTE" as cigarette smoking becomes more popular.

1915: American Tobacco Company removes the R.A. Patterson name from the Lucky Strike logo and continues putting out roll cut tins, now with hinges. The once popular brand begins to languish in sales.

or cigars. Then when smoking replaced chewing and snuffing as the more popular method of tobacco use, Lucky Strike changed to a rolled cut, which was much easier to smoke than cut plug, which was more suited to chewing. Gradually the Rolled Cut became an even finer "Crimp Cut" as cigarettes replaced pipe and cigar smoking. Finally, factory-rolled

1916: The factory-rolled Lucky Strike cigarette makes its debut, designed to compete head-to-head with Camel. In the days before soft packs and cardboard cartons, cigarettes were purchased in tin drums of 100 (or purchased singly from an open drum at the retailer's counter) and carried around inside a cigarette holder. Roll-your-owners still had the roll-cut version to work with.

1920: A more practical container appeared on the market: the "Flat Fifties" case. This tin held 50 cigarettes and was designed to fit flatly in a suit pocket.

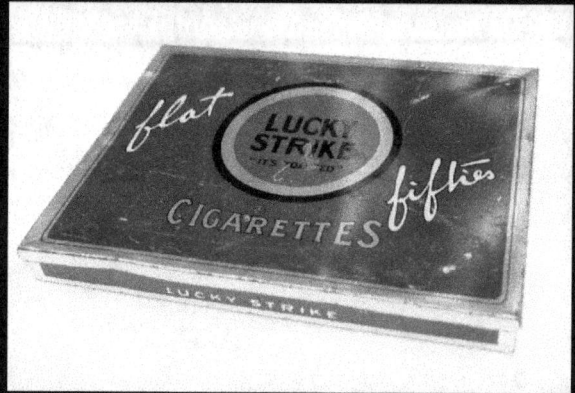

1922: Finally, somebody invented the twenty pack paper case that remains the standard to this day. Cellophane wrapping and cardboard cartons would come a bit later.

1925: Lucky Strike Roll Cut is paired with Buckingham Cut Plug and sold as "Half & Half"- for pipe and cigarette.

1936: Lucky Strike pack receives its first real redesign. The scheme is basically the same but the word CIGARETTES is streamlined at the bottom of the pack and the gold coloring is substituted for white. Other than that, everything remains the same until WWII.

1942: Lucky Strike goes white. First up was the roll-your-own tin:

cigarettes were brought out in 1915 and have been manufactured ever since. The twenties saw the birth of Half & Half smoking tobacco, which was comprised of 50% Lucky Strike Roll Cut and 50% Buckingham Cut Plug. It, too is manufactured to this day, albeit without the Lucky Strike brand affiliation. The Lucky pack went white during WWII. The 60's, 80's and 90's saw failed attempts at launching filtered versions of both Lucky Strikes and Half and Half that met with little success. Brown and Williamson was then bought by RJ Reynolds who have yet to attempt a revival of the filtered version. With the decline of smoking, Lucky Strike is launched as a Swedish Snus brand in 2006 with a dedicated, loyal following .

1943:The transformation is complete, and the new Lucky Strike design is arguable the most recognizable cigarette pack of all time.

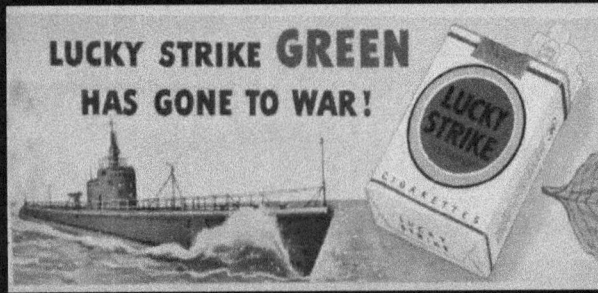

1955: The Half & Half can cuts its historic branding and the "Lucky Strike" and "Buckingham" logos are replaced with slogans. Roll Cut RYO Lucky Strike disappears for good.

1964: Lucky now comes in a filtered version, menthol version, and menthol 100.

1965: Half and Half: The Pipe Tobacco Cigarette.

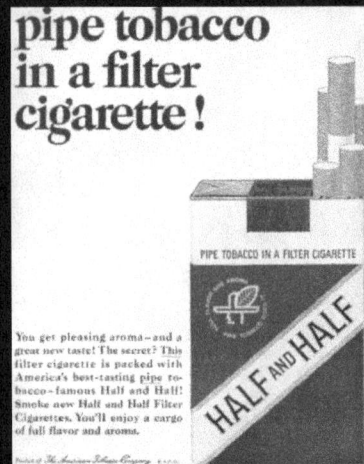

1967: Lucky Strike 100s: "The Lucky Strike that doesn't taste like a Lucky Strike."

1986: Lucky Strike filters are brought back, this time with a Light version. The brand received slight renewed interest due to Don Johnson's character on *Miami Vice* smoking them.

1989: The Lucky filters line is canceled again and replaced with Half & Half cigarettes, available in regular and 100 lengths. It too is canceled in less than a year.

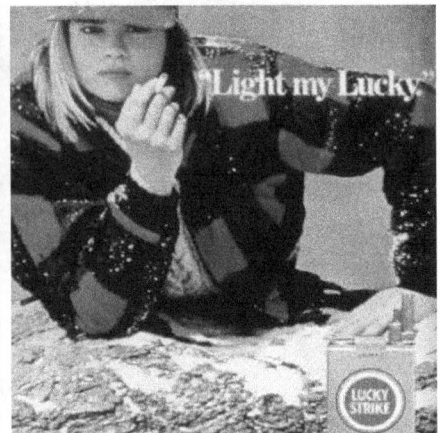

46

1997-1999: Lucky Strike filters are revived again, this time in Regular, 100, Lights, and Light 100s.

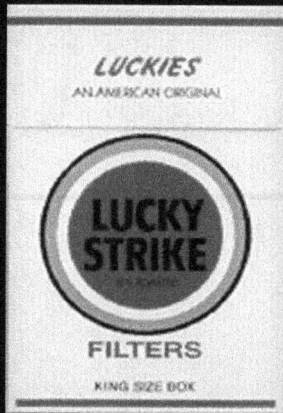

2004: RJ Reynolds buys out Brown and Williamson. The Lucky Brand is no longer a competitor to Camel non-filters, but a stablemate.

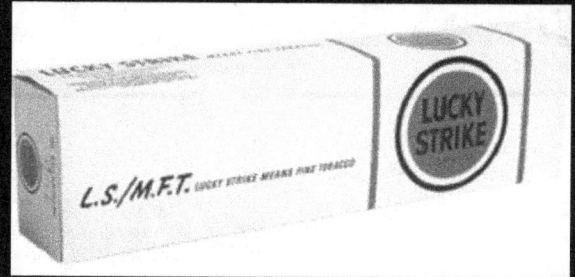

2006- Present: Lucky Strike Swedish Snus is introduced to worldwide acclaim. Distributed by BAT in Scandinavia, the brand is quickly imported by American snusers, who are thrilled at having a premium snus with a brand name that they recognize.

2010: RJ Reynolds, who owns the Lucky Strike brand in the USA, files an injunction against snus shops for copyright infringement and American snusers are no longer able to legally import it into this country.

Present: Half & Half is still widely available all over the US, sold in the pouch pack and bulk plastic tub.

Present: Lucky Strike cigarettes remain hugely popular throughout Europe and Asia. In the USA, they are mainly smoked by pretentious douchebag hipsters.

<u>To</u> g<u>ive</u> y<u>ou</u>
<u>a</u> <u>finer</u> <u>cigarette</u>

Lucky Strike maintains

AMERICA'S FINEST CIG

Largest and most fully equipped cigarette research laboratory in America is your guarantee that Luckies are a finer cigarette!

YOU SEE HERE the largest and most complete laboratory of its kind operated by any cigarette manufacturer in America.

For many years Lucky Strike scientists have delved into cigarette research on an extensive scale. Out of this has grown an elaborate system of quality control. Every step in the making of Luckies—from before the tobacco is bought until the finished cigarette reaches you—comes under the laboratory's watchful eye. As you read this, a constant stream of tobacco . . . samples from every tobacco-growing area . . . is flowing into the laboratory in Richmond, Virginia. These samples are scientifically analyzed, and reports of their quality go to the men who buy at auction for the makers of Lucky Strike.

Armed with this confidential, scientific information—and their own sound judgment—these men go after finer tobacco. This fine tobacco—together with scientifically controlled manufacturing methods—is your assurance that there is no finer, more enjoyable cigarette than Lucky Strike!

So round, so firm, so fully packed. Typical of many special devices designed to maintain the highest standards of cigarette quality, this mechanism helps to avoid loose ends . . . makes doubly sure your Lucky is so round, so firm, so fully packed.

So free and easy on the draw. This meter draws air through the cigarette, measures the draw. Samples are tested to see if they are properly filled. Tests like this one are your guarantee that the Luckies you smoke are truly free and easy on the draw.

Why Luckies smoke evenly—not too fast, not too slow. This apparatus, together with many other technical devices, evaluates the smoking qualities of a cigarette — guarantees that your Lucky Strike smokes properly—smoothly and evenly.

In its 160 year history as a premium tobacco product, Lucky Strike has always been known for its groundbreaking, sometimes controversial ads. Here are some of the most memorable.

Circa 1907.

IS THIS YOU FIVE YEARS FROM NOW?

When tempted to over-indulge

"Reach for a Lucky instead"

"It's toasted"

Your Throat Protection — against irritation — against

"To stay slender—

reach for a Lucky

"It's toasted"

To keep a slender figure
No one can deny…

Reach
for a
LUCKY
instead of a
sweet

"It's toasted"

"Light a Lucky
and you'll never miss sweets
that make you fat"

Constance Talmadge,
Charming Motion
Picture Star

"REACH FOR A LUCKY
INSTEAD OF A SWEET."

"It's toasted"

No Throat Irritation—No Cough.

FACE THE FACTS!

When tempted to over-indulge

"Reach for a Lucky instead"

1931: Gender Equality.

Be moderate—be moderate in all things, even in smoking. Avoid that future shadow * by avoiding over-indulgence, if you would maintain that modern, ever-youthful figure. "Reach for a Lucky instead."

Lucky Strike, the finest Cigarette you ever smoked, made of the finest tobacco—The Cream of the Crop—"IT'S TOASTED." **Lucky Strike** has an extra, secret heating process. Everyone knows that heat purifies and so 20,679 physicians say that **Luckies** are less irritating to your throat.

LUCKY STRIKE "IT'S TOASTED"

CIGARETTES

"It's toasted"

Your Throat Protection — against irritation — against cough.

*We do not say smoking **Luckies** reduces flesh. We do say when tempted to over-indulge, "Reach for a **Lucky** instead."

LUCKY STRIKE **GREEN** HAS GONE TO WAR!

So here's the smart new uniform for fine tobacco

THE *Cigarette* THAT'S *Winning* THE WAR

USE Victory Bread SAVE WHEAT

USE Victory Bread—save wheat. That's our important obligation with you now.

When you have it toasted—just right, and buttered too, you'll find that this "substitute" bread has a lot more flavor.

Toasting brings out flavor—every time. It makes tobacco delicious. Try Lucky Strike Cigarettes—it's toasted.

LUCKY STRIKE CIGARETTE

It's toasted

HELP OUR BOYS *TOAST* HITLER **BUY WAR BONDS**

Right: One of the rarest Lucky Ads of all time. A screaming blonde is being carted off by two conquerors, who are apparently about to "roughly" double rape her. The tagline "Nature in the raw is seldom mild... and raw tobaccos have no place in cigarettes" caused quite a stir and the ad was quickly withdrawn.

—and raw tobaccos have no place in cigarettes

It's toasted

The 1960's: Mixed Up Confusion

Remember how great cigarettes used to taste?

LUCKIES STILL DO

AWARD-WINNING CONCERT COMPOSER ULYSSES KAY has been smoking Luckies for years and wouldn't switch for the world. "Luckies are the best-tasting cigarette I ever smoked," he says. Try a pack yourself. A Lucky's sweet to your taste.

L.S./M.F.T.—Lucky Strike Means Fine Tobacco

TOBACCO AND TASTE TOO FINE TO FILTER

Product of The American Tobacco Company—"Tobacco is our middle name"

Lucky Strike introduces the Lucky Strike that doesn't taste like a Lucky Strike.

"Show me a filter that really delivers taste and I'll eat my hat!"

New Lucky Strike Filters

put back the taste others take away

L.S./M.F.T.—Lucky Strike means fine tobacco...and now Lucky Strike means filter tip. So you get—unchanged—Lucky's famous fine-tobacco blend. And Lucky's filter tip actually

Now there are 2 Lucky Strikes that don't taste like a Lucky Strike.

The 1970's: The "Old Fart" Cigarette

The 70's were the worst decade yet for Lucky Strike. Their filtered version flopped and try as they might, they couldn't get the younger crowd to smoke their Grandfather's cigarette. Attempting to compete with Marlboro's "manly men doing manly things" theme, a few ads appeared in 1970 that, in all honesty, smacked of homoerotic undertones. Lucky Strike ads virtually disappeared for another 15 years.

Get the genuine article

End to end it's fine tobacco

Get the honest taste of a Lucky Strike

The 1980's: Metrosexual Miami Vice Ads

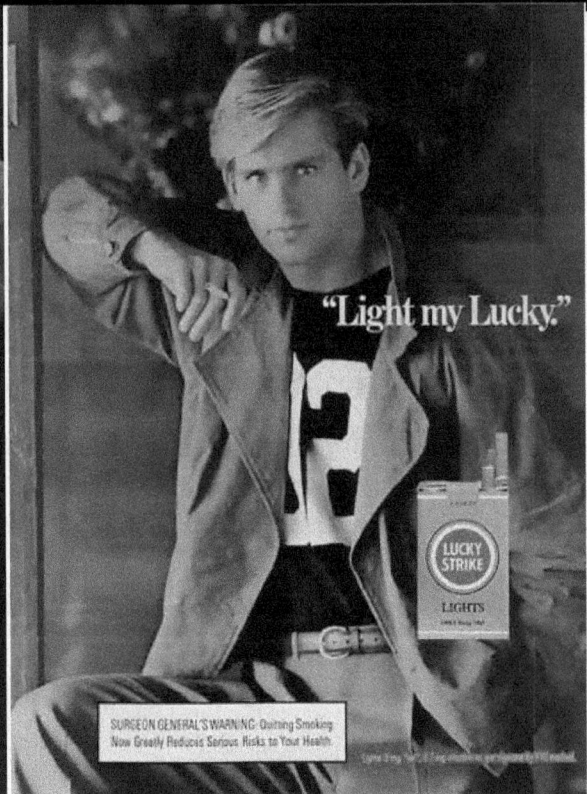

"Light my Lucky."

LUCKY STRIKE

LIGHTS

SURGEON GENERAL'S WARNING: Cigarette Smoke Contains Carbon Monoxide.

"Light my Lucky."

LUCKY STRIKE

LIGHTS

SURGEON GENERAL'S WARNING: Quitting Smoking Now Greatly Reduces Serious Risks to Your Health.

In 1986, B&W attempted a new line of filtered Luckies. The brand had renewed interest when Don Johnson's character in *Miami Vice* occasionally smoked the non-filtered version. Unfortunately, the fad was short-lived and had disappeared by 1990, by which time it had become a bargain brand. The last ad attempted to capture the nostalgia factor of smoking such an historic cigarette, but it was too late. The writing was on the wall.

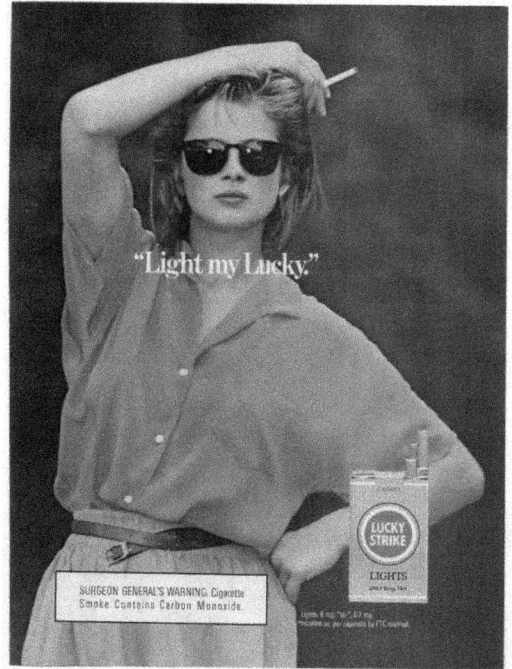

Sales of Lucky Strike had really begun to take off in Europe during the 90's, especially in Germany and East Europe. In 1997, following the short nostalgia wave in the US that began with *Pulp Fiction* and ended with Swing Dancing, Lucky Strike filters were once again introduced. They were gone by 2001.

IMPORTED
LUCKY STRIKE
SOFT PACK.

I CHOOSE
AN AMERICAN ORIGINAL

WARNING: CIGARETTE SMOKING IS DANGEROUS TO HEALTH

Seien Sie dekadent.
Rauchen Sie Antiquitäten.

Rauchen kann tödlich sein

Lucky Strike. Sonst nichts.

Translation: "Be decadent. Smoke an antique." German RYO "Fireleaf."

The Euro ad that made headlines around the world. The "I Choose" campaign of 2005 featured an ad with two women getting ready to lock lips. People either loved it or hated it, but Lucky Strike sales went through the roof.

I CHOOSE
AN AMERICAN ORIGINAL

When Lucky Strike snus was launched in 2006, BAT decided to forgo traditional media ads and instead promote their products inside clubs and restaurants with extravagant point-of-sale displays.

Lucky Strike is still a well known brand to this day, thanks to a thriving European following, a first-class snus product, and a hipster obsession fueled in part by *Mad Men*'s Don Draper being rarely seen without a Lucky hanging out of his mouth.

What will the next 160 years of Lucky Strike ads hold in store? Hopefully more hot lesbians and less guys wearing aviator sunglasses and Members Only bomber jackets.

STRANGE...
BUT TRUE !

TOBACCO-RELATED ODDITIES AND ANECDOTES

COMPILED BY DAVID THIGPEN

Blowing Smoke Up Your...

Right: A "Tobacco Bellows Kit" by London's Evans & Co, circa 1834.

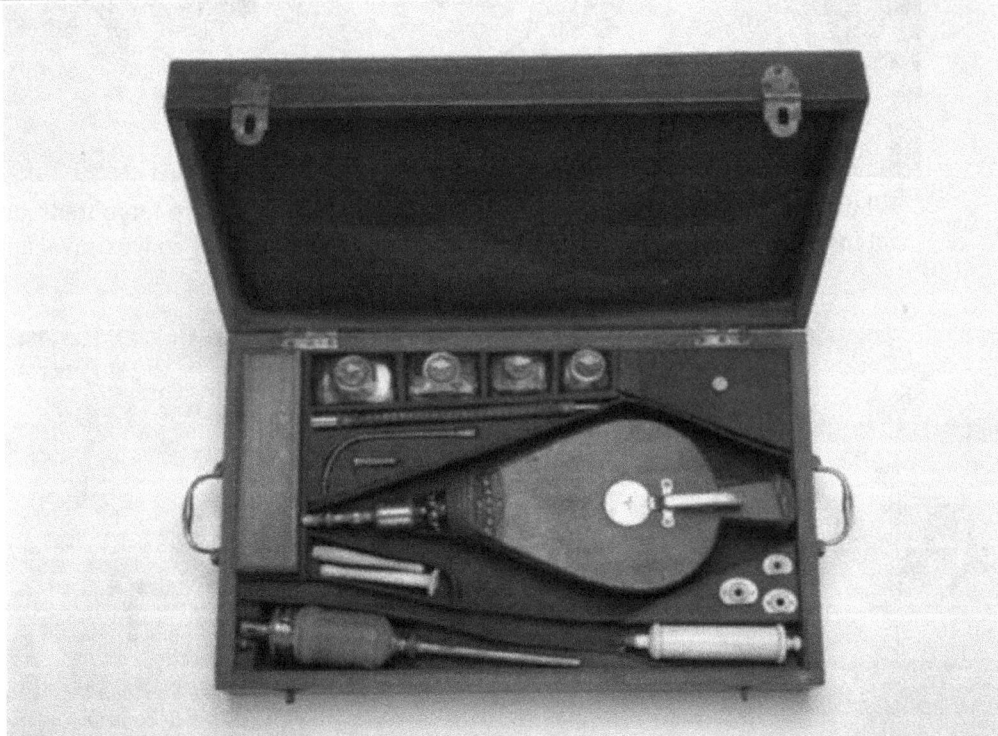

Almost as long as mankind has chewed, snuffed or smoked tobacco, he has been sticking it in his rectum. Some Indian tribes did it in order to bring forth hallucinations, while others used it more practically to treat hemorrhoids and piles. There was a resurgence in the popularity of tobacco enemas during the Victorian period, when all manner of disease was thought to be treatable by a bellows apparatus that blew tobacco smoke directly into one's bowels by way of the anus. The craze died out after about 100 years worth of no noticeable results. Historians claim that this is the root of the phrase "blowing smoke up one's arse," which remains in modern usage some 200 years after it originated.

Prince Randian, the "Freak" that broke world records

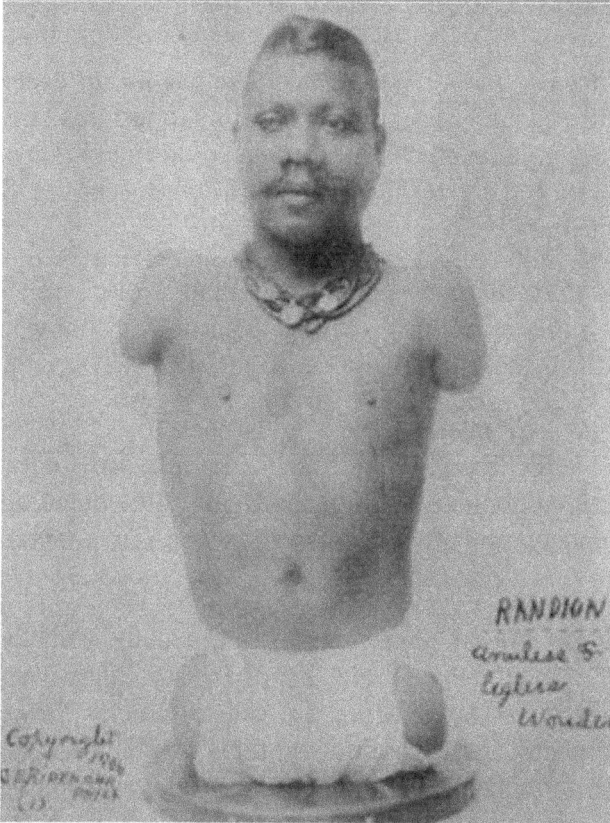

RANDION
armless &
legless
Wonder

Copyright
1934
...

Last issue we mentioned the 1932 film *Freaks* and its director, Tod Browning, whose screen version of *Dracula* stunned audiences worldwide the year before. *Freaks* was an unexpected bomb however; it was banned in most countries until the 1960's and surviving prints today are still heavily censored. Public outrage over the use of real sideshow performers in the movie was misdirected- the sideshow performers are portrayed as being just as normal as you and I, whereas the two "normal" performers are misanthropic monsters who prey on the kindness of the circus freaks. But audiences of 1932 were just not ready for such a radical concept, and the movie was quickly swept under the rug.

One of the stars of the film was Prince Randian, an Indian-born father of five who spoke six languages. Randian went under dozens of other stage names throughout his long and distinguished career. "The Snake Man" (or, as he preferred to call himself, "The Human Torso") had no arms or legs but could perform marvelous feats using only his mouth and lips. His most famous stunt, featured in *Freaks*, was the cigarette trick.

His cigarette trick took less than 40 seconds to pull off (a world record that stands to this day.) Using only his lips, teeth and tongue, Randian would pull a rolling paper out of the pack, open a pouch of tobacco and sprinkle the contents into the empty paper, roll it into a cylinder and lick it sealed. He would then pull a match out of a box and light it, place the lit match on the cover of the box, and position his cigarette towards the flame. He then rolled the cigarette into the corner of his mouth and use his tongue to extinguish the match.

He was said to be the fastest of such "limbless lighters," a popular subcategory of the Sideshow era. (Sadly, his performance in *Freaks* was edited down to feature only the match lighting part of the trick and any excised footage has long since gone missing.)

A most remarkable man, Randian could do virtually anything a limbed man could do, include shave with a razor, cook on a stove, draw, paint, write, and do yardwork. His wife remembered walking into the toolshed one morning to find her husband cutting wood with the handle of a full-sized saw clamped firmly in his teeth. Unlike many other sideshow performers of his time, Randian loved his work and commanded a large salary. A devout Christian, he died in his New Jersey home on December 19th, 1934 just a few hours after his farewell performance at the world famous 14th Street Museum. "I am retiring," he told that crowd. "There are many places I wish to visit now."

Did You Know? The popular children's show "Yo Gabba Gabba" was named in tribute to the Ramones, whose song "Pinhead" contained the refrain "*Gabba Gabba we accept you, we accept you, one of us.*" That line was taken from the movie *Freaks*, which Dee Dee and Joey Ramone had seen in a Times Square grindhouse theater during an early seventies revival.

Urban Legend Dept.

In honor of the 160th anniversary festivities this issue, we take a look at one of the most fabled brands in all tobaccodom: Lucky Strike.

- *Back when marijuana was legal, they called the brand "Lucky Strike" because one out of every 20 cigarettes in the pack was actually a joint.* Unfortunately for stoners who like to tell this tale, the name "Lucky Strike" was in reference to striking gold, as the brand originated during the days of the American Gold Rush. (This legend was also started about the cartons of Luckies sent to US troops in WWII, except that the ratio was now 1 one out 200.)

- *Lucky Strikes were uniquely "toasted," owing to their distinctive taste.* Actually, all cigarette tobacco is "toasted" to some degree, even today, so this was just marketing hyperbole. There was nothing significantly different, manufacture wise, from any other American cigarette of the era.

- *Lucky Strikes were the first cigarette marketed directly to women.* This is open to debate, as Marlboro cigarettes "Mild as May" campaign was launched roughly at the same time that Lucky Strike's "Reach for a Lucky instead of a Sweet" gained popularity. Both ads were groundbreaking for their time, but Lucky Strike's proved to be the most popular of the two and is well-remembered even today.

- *Lucky Strike was sued by the candy industry over the "Sweet" campaign.* It's true that the candy industry was furious over the "Reach for a Lucky Instead of a Sweet" ads, mainly because they were so successful. The sales of chocolate and candies went down while the sale of Lucky Strike skyrocketed. The American Confectioners Union appealed to the government for help, claiming that the tobacco industry was promoting cigarettes as being "safe and slimming" while candy was touted as being "dangerous and fattening." American Tobacco voluntarily pulled the ads, though the threat of litigation was never actually carried out.

- *The Green packaging of Lucky Strike was changed to white to help with the war effort.* More marketing hyperbole. In research studies, the color green was determined to be out of fashion with young women, who were wearing more and more whites and beiges. This helped explain why Lucky Strike's popularity with men remained steady while women were switching to brands with white packaging, like Chesterfield and Philip Morris Commanders.

  It was decided that something drastic needed to be done to retain female smokers, so the ad execs came up with the perfect idea: redesign the pack and claim that the green coloring was being rationed for the war. The new "white" Lucky pack was created by design genius Raymond Loewy and was quite striking, the red "bullseye" on a flat white background. By explaining that the green ink was being "sacrificed" for our boys over in WWII, it also made American Tobacco look like a patriotic company. The new pack proved so popular that Lucky Strike once again rose to dominate the market, which it had been battling with Chesterfield and Camel for years.

- *There was a leper working in the Lucky Strike factory.* Although this story has been associated with every major pre-filtered cigarette brand at one time or another (including Lucky Strike), it reached its peak popularity with the Chesterfield brand in 1934. It was an outright lie circulated by insiders at competing cigarette companies and it severely damaged the reputation of Ligget & Myers (Chesterfield's parent company), who were also busy trying to combat rumors that it was linked to the Nazi party over in Germany (also untrue).

- *The Green Pack was changed to White during WWII at Harry Truman's behest, in order to celebrate the bombing of Hiroshima. The red "sun" on white is meant to signify the Japanese flag, and the word "Strike" alluded to its bombing.* As already explained, the pack was changed because the color green was considered out of fashion with women. Also, the color change occurred before the Hiroshima bombings, so Truman had to have had an itchy trigger finger and everyone at American Tobacco was able to keep the most important secret in the world under wraps.

- *L.S./M.F.T. stands for something racist, pornographic, or satanic.* The designation L.S./M.F.T., found at the bottom of every pack, was short for **Lucky Strike Means Fine Tobacco**, a popular tagline of its day.

- *During various wars, American soldiers were ordered to smoke Lucky Strikes (and other non-filter cigarettes) backwards.* The reasoning was that if the enemy came upon a cigarette butt, they wouldn't know if it was from an American GI or from one of their own men, since the logo of the cigarette had been burned off. (The Lucky Strike logo would have been a dead giveaway that US Troops had been in the area). This rumor has never been substantiated, but it's often told by veterans who served in WWII and Korea.

- *The "lucky" cigarette superstition started with Lucky Strike.* The practice of designating the first cigarette out of the pack as a "lucky" cigarette to be turned upside down and smoked last may have started with Lucky Strike, but nobody knows for sure. Since the custom didn't become popular until filtered cigarettes were packaged in flip top boxes late into the 1960's, it's probably not true.

- *"Sold!" was an expression that originated with Lucky Strike.* Picture this familiar scenario: a man at a yard sale haggles with the seller over the price of a toaster. The seller sweetens the deal by throwing in a free set of headphones. The buyer, unable to resist, exclaims "Sold!" and hands over his three dollars.

   This expression actually did originate with Lucky Strike tobacco auctions, where the auctioneer rattled off his prices to the bidders, culminating in the famous line, "SOLD! American!" This became a catchphrase of sorts during the 1930s and exists today, although the "American" part is usually absent.

- *If you called the 1-800 number on the side of the Lucky Strike pack, you got a very strange recording.* This one is true, believe it or not. In the late 90's, shortly before RJR bought out Brown and Williamson, B&W experimented with an early viral marketing ploy to get internet users buzzing. If you dialed the 800 number on the Lucky pack, you got a strange, slightly disturbing message delivered in an deadpan Don Draper-type monotone.

   "We, the Brown & Williamson Tobacco Corporation, are in love with you. Yep, you heard right. Brown & Williamson Tobacco is in love. We're a giant corporation, and you make us feel like a little kitten. Thank you, lover." The viral marketing seemed to backfire, though. Most Generation X internet users (presumably the target of this type of ad), rather than finding the message buzz-worthy, were surprised that Lucky Strike cigarettes were still being manufactured more than anything else.

- *Malcolm X once said that the only thing he liked about white people was that they invented Lucky Strike cigarettes.* While it's true that he smoked Lucky Strikes, the source of this rumor has never been verifiable. It would make a great viral marketing campaign though!

Smoking = Dangerous, Snuff = Safe

Almost 400 years ago, the British Government recognized the safety of snuff compared to smoking.

The first recorded tobacco smoking accident occurred in 1623. While celebrating the return of a Jamestown relief ship in Bermuda, the sailors on deck pulled out their pipes and alcohol and partied like it was 1699. Some hapless drunk dropped his lit pipe, which rolled below deck to the gunpowder store. The flames ignited the barrels of gunpowder and the ship blew up, killing or wounding everyone onboard.

Such later incidents caused the Royal Navy to issue a decree that banned the smoking of tobacco on ships carrying explosives, and so the Dutch Cavendish favored so highly at the time was traded in for Spanish snuff and the chewing quid. The popular image of the sailor with a meerschaum pipe forever clenched in his mouth was a bit of revisionist history; nearly all of the seamen in the British, Spanish, French (and later the American) Navies almost exclusively used snuff while onboard. In fact, lighting a match on deck for the purpose of smoking was once an executable offense under some Naval codes.

Snuff: The Key to Manhood

The ancient Amazonian tribe of the Tucanos, like most indigenous people, had certain rituals in place that marked the transition from boyhood to manhood. In a lavish ceremony, horns and drums were blown and banged, and the young man was given a bone box filled with very potent, almost hallucinogenic snuff. If the boy was able to handle the snuff and recite the proper vows and prayers, he was deemed a man and enjoyed all the benefits that adulthood held for the Tucano tribesmen (mainly going hunting and the right to have sex with his sister if he saw fit.)

If the youth was unable to handle the effects of the powerful snuff, he was banished from the village and shamed into not returning. His only hope was to join another tribe or live a solitary existence in the wilds of the Amazon.

Crazy, Man, Crazy

Little is heard today of the Scottish physician Dr. Lennox Johnston, but he was one of the first modern researchers to pinpoint nicotine as the primary cause of addiction in tobacco users.

Though Johnston himself smoked for 12 years, he quit immediately after determining through epidemiological research that cigarettes caused lung cancer. (He also proposed, quite wrongly, that snuffing caused emphysema and cancer of the sinuses.) Johnston then began what in 1942 was a very lonely crusade: a total ban on all tobacco sales and use. He discovered that by injecting smokers with pure nicotine, he was able to break their addictions. (Lennox himself almost died on six separate occasions testing the nicotine on himself.) However, the British Medical Association refused to publish his findings, and he threatened to blow up their offices, which caused him to be committed to an insane asylum for a short while and all of his studies to be discredited.

His career never recovered and despite later studies that proved most of his theories correct, Johnston died in relative obscurity in 1986.

STE

BLACKGUARD OF THE MONTH□

PAMELA MCCOLL

Pamela McColl made headlines late October when she announced her "cleaned-up" publication of Clement Clarke Moore's 1822 poem "'Twas the Night Before Christmas," also known as "A Visit From St. Nicholas." The beloved American classic, which millions of families still read aloud on Christmas Eve, offended the Canadian publisher so much that she axed two lines referencing Santa's tobacco addiction:

'The stump of a pipe he held tight in his teeth, / And the smoke, it encircled his head like a wreath.'

The familiar title illustration showing the offending pipe was also cut from this release. The screwed up Canuck explained that she was attempting to "save lives and avoid influencing new smokers". The American Library Association shot back with a statement saying "Such censorship misrepresents the artist's original work and relies wholly on the idea that children are incapable of critical thinking or that a parent's guidance and training are meaningless," claimed Deborah Caldwell-Stone, deputy director of the ALA's office for intellectual freedom.

Marilu Henner (left) slumming it up with Pamela McColl, holding a copy of her infamous "PC" *Night Before Christmas.*

McColl defended her biased censorship by saying that her cuts did not distract from the "material intent of the author nor do they infringe on the reader's understanding or enjoyment of this historically-rich story."

She then added that "I think these edits outweigh other considerations. If this text is to survive another 200 years it needs to modernize and reflect today's realities. I want children to celebrate the spirit of giving and to reflect proudly on the holiday traditions that shape their childhood, and the best way to honor Santa and this story is to make him smoke-free." (If a poem is "historically rich", then why does it need to be "modernized"?)

Well Pam, if you can use your publishing company to poop on "*'Twas the night*" with your anti-tobacco bias, we aim to set things right by using *our* publishing company to put out the original uncensored, un-PC edition. And if you *truly* want to "celebrate the spirit of giving," we challenge you to do the same thing Lucien Publishing will do with our version by donating all of the profits to charity. We'll even pick an organization of your choice. Merry Christmas, you horrible, despicable ****.

The Snuff Taker's Ephemeris *is offering the families of our readers a chance to own an alternate version of* "'Twas The Night Before Christmas" *featuring the unexpurgated original text of the poem accompanied by historical "Tobacco Santa" illustrations reprinted from previous editions.*

This printing will be limited to 500 copies with all profits going to charity. See our ad later in this issue for more details.

When pressed for comment, a clearly annoyed Santa simple responded: "Don't worry. I know where the bitch lives."

THE SNUFF TAKER'S EPHEMERIS

Presents:

The Five Sexiest Men Alive

"People" picked Channing Tatum, N. Korea picked Kim Jong-un. See who WE picked as the world's sexiest males/anti-tobacco nuts.

5. Barack Obama

With those sociopath-Sammy Davis Jr. good looks and that "just don't give a damn" demeanor, we can be assured that over the next four years, America will be treated to the sexiest anti- tobacco legislation and smokin' HAWT tax rates that we've come to love since 2008.

4. John Dalli

Good golly, John Dalli! You just have to admire a man with testicles large enough to serve as the head of the EU's Tobacco Control Initiative while simultaneously trying to extort cash from Swedish Match. VAT a catch!

3. Stanton Glantz

At first Glantz, you might not think that old Stan here could hold his own against the other hunks on this list, but get this: Glantz has been lying about the effects of tobacco use in order to further his own financial and personal gains since 1978! That's five decades of decadence. Eat that, Myers!

2. Matt Myers

This CEO of Tobacco Free Kids is dead sexy. And if you're a smoker that believes his propaganda that paints smokeless tobacco as being just as dangerous as cigarette smoking, *you'll* be dead too! Smokeless is 98% safer than smoking- but we know how easy it is to be deceived by such a stud muffin.

1. Henry Waxman

Was there really ever any competition? Whether he's pushing the biggest anti-tobacco legislation ever levied against the American people into law or outside on the lawn, washing and waxing his pristine '86 Fiero, there's no denying the pure, charismatic sex appeal that oozes off of Hank "The Plank" Waxman. "Henry is the epitome of masculinity," claims Secretary of State Hillary Clinton. "He's who I've tried to model myself after, both physically *and* politically."

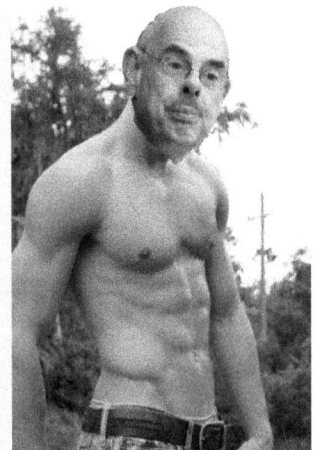

ƧTƧ

Secondhand Snus Is a Real Thing

Commentary by Anthony Haddad

Most snusers will tell you that one of the benefits of snus is that there is no "secondhand" snus. That's not quite true. Secondhand snusing is real.

But I'm not sure secondhand smoke is a bad thing. I mean, you get pissed at your kid, and you just blow some smoke in his face. That's much nicer than whacking that little dipshit in the head with a cricket bat. I don't have a kid, but I do have a dog. If I smoked, I'd blow secondhand smoke in his face if he shit on the rug. Or if you had a wife, you could blow smoke in her face when she shits on the rug. I don't have a wife, but I do have sex workers. When they shit on the rug, I have to pay more.

Blowing smoke in someone's face holds a nice midpoint between a middle finger and a slap. The middle finger is too pedestrian. Try driving two miles down the road and not getting a middle finger – it's impossible. And a slap could have the pigs ringing your doorbell. Smoke in the face is like saying to someone, "You're pissing me off, but you're too much of a dog/wife for me to beat."

But you can secondhand snus. It's just requires you to get a lot closer to the other person than smoke. Imagine you have prime rib for dinner and then go boff a vegetarian. That's called secondhand prime rib, and she can no longer say she hasn't eaten meat since the 90s anymore. Or if you eat a bunch of crab at the buffet and then swap spit with a homeless guy in the alley, it's practically like buying him dinner – secondhand crab.

Most cases of oral herpes in the last ten years are directly attributable to the large number of snusers that attend so-called "Crackwhore Renaissance Fairs" that have sprung up throughout the American Southwest.

You may scoff at this idea, but it has been proven in custom and law with peanut butter. If you know your girlfriend will die if she gets nuts in her mouth, and you chow down a box of Planters before you stick your face in her crotch – congratulations – you're now a murderer.

Secondhand snus works similarly. If you go mouth to mouth, mouth to genitals, mouth to anus or mouth to open wound on someone while snusing, they are getting secondhand snus. Basic etiquette dictates that you should inform your counterpart of any snus in your mouth before undertaking such activities.

Anthony "Festering Maw" Haddad blogs about snus over at Drsnus.com.

How Far Can "Too Far" Go?

An op-ed by Catherine DeMarsh

I am sure I am not the only tobacco user who has heard from their doctor, their friends, or family, maybe even a few co-workers, "You should quit smoking." Or, "Smoking is such a nasty habit." Or the million and a half dozen other nasty little comments which non-tobacco users say to make you and I feel self conscious about our tobacco use. Well, I'm not sure about what *you* say to these people, but I tend to answer them generally with a sweet smile and say, "I smoke to keep the homicide rate down. And when I can't smoke I will use my Swedish snus. Just realize, harassing me about my tobacco use could be hazardous to YOUR health."

I have written several articles for SnusCentral.com about how our government has become more and more of a 'Nanny State.' Of how they take our tobacco tax money which we are told is to be spent on X,Y and Z is borrowed against and instead, spent on pet projects of the various politicians who claim to be in office protecting all of his or her constituents. Funny how I, as a tobacco user, find they are happy to tax the hell out of my "pursuit of happiness," and in turn, I find my rights to that happiness slowly being taken away.

Anti- tobacco-Nazis started their war on my rights by saying they were trying to "Save the Children." In 1987, the drinking age was raised from 18 to 21, and to even enter a bar you have to be 21, which by all rights makes you an adult, yet to "Save the Children" many states have banned smoking in bars. If you compare the numbers, the alcohol served in bars has done more to kill people than the tobacco being used. Think about it… not just what the alcohol itself does to the body, by slowly eroding the liver as well as kidneys, but secondhand drunkenness is more deadly than secondhand smoke. (Don't believe me? Ask the thousands of people who lost a family member this year when a drunk crossed the center line and killed their loved one.)

Recently I came across some information I really thought was out of this world, over the top, fully biased, and now proof of what our government thinks of tobacco users by allowing employers to treat us as second class citizens. I couldn't believe they could legally get away with it, but after talking to a couple of lawyers and doing some checking on my own I found that in the state of Ohio it is legal for employers to test and deny employment based on nicotine use. And Ohio is not alone; several other states have in laws like this in place or are considering them. Now unfortunately, this also means *any* nicotine use, which includes the patch, gum and pharmaceutical products that the anti-tobacco-Nazis want people to use instead of tobacco.

A few years ago Ohioans voted to allow gambling in some of the race tracks and in the form of major casinos to be built in, around or near the four major cities in Ohio (Cleveland, Toledo, Columbus, and Cincinnati). Although Ohio had become a smoke-free state a few years before (meaning a ban on lighting up within enclosed public places), this is the first time I have heard of having to be tobacco-free, or in this case, *nicotine*-free as being a condition of employment.

According to one of the hiring managers for the Toledo Hollywood Casino:

Applicants will be asked if they use any sort of tobacco product on their initial application. However, Herndon warns it is not worth lying. "Once you do move further in the process, when we do our drug testing, we also test for tobacco use. So even if you're not 100 percent honest on the application, we'll still find it out later." Applicants who fail the drug test can apply again in six months to prove they no longer have nicotine or drugs in their systems.

The last I checked, tobacco was still a legal substance. But not according to some employers. I can understand testing for illegal substances, but legal ones? And then denying employment because of it? As I read an article from the Columbus Dispatch about the hiring of employees in the new Columbus Hollywood Casino, I continued to ask myself, "Where does it end?" Are they willing to deny employment due to alcohol use? What about people who use aspirin? Tylenol? People who have low iron? Or maybe they are diabetic? *Where does it end?* Where would the ACLU be if Wal-Mart suddenly decided that they wouldn't hire women who have ever had abortions, since it doesn't fit into their "moral code of decency"? But, as nicotine users, we're fairly used to being made the scapegoat for all of society's ills.

Here's the inside scoop from one unlucky(?) applicant, Gino Bowles:

I Interviewed with Hollywood Casino yesterday who informed me that they were a "tobacco free" company. Under the guise of "promoting health" they are getting major insurance breaks because of having a non-smoking staff. Now, I understand smoking is bad, but people have been fired under random drug tests because they test for nicotine as well. Even as a user of a patch or gum or e-cig you'd be terminated.

I was later emailed a notice that I had a second interview that I declined, stating: "Thank you for your consideration, but I have chosen to withdraw my application from Hollywood Casino. Despite my dislike of cigarettes, I refuse to support a company that discriminates against those who smoke amidst an economic downturn. Be well." My question is, how long before caffeine, a night out drinking or obesity becomes a fireable offense? Those are all insurance risks also and I fear through the small battles won, we lose more and more rights.

I would like to give kudos to Gino Bowles, for standing up and being heard. For understanding how slippery a slope this is. He could have just said nothing and got a well-paying job with great health benefits in the new Columbus casino where no one uses tobacco, er, nicotine. Jobs with benefits like these are few and far between even in the best of times, but in today's economy they are more like miracles. Mr. Bowles stood up not only for his principals but for the rights of his fellow citizens. That takes balls, something that many of us lack.

The Hollywood Casino (left), Columbus Ohio. Nicotine users not welcome.

Paradoxically, you may notice the giant portrait of actress Zsa Zsa Gabor, who at age 95 still smokes a pack a day and has done so for the last 80 years.

There is a coffee chain in Oakland, Canada that decided to go smoke free. Tim Horton's Coffee, instead of tearing out the old building material and replacing everything– air conditioning system, vents, filters and all required machinery– decided that it would be more cost effective to build a brand new shop right across the street on a competing corner. They knew there was going to be some adjusting as people, shifts and things were transferred to the new store. They pulled people from other stores and from corporate to fill in positions until they could transition to the new store.

At first it was thought that the revenue from the original store would be split between the two stores, as the new location would struggle financially for the first several months. But as the new smoke-free Horton's showed itself as being more than capable of holding its own, the old store also experienced a rise in profits. In a most unusual decision, Horton's decided to keep both stores, the smoking and non-smoking shops, running side by side. Therefore, a non-smoker that walks into the "Old" Tim Horton's needs merely to walk across the street in order to receive the same great coffee and breakfast, albeit in a smoke-free environment. Everyone was happy because a balance was struck.

In the state of Ohio, OSHA recommends:

- At least one half hour break and two fifteen minute breaks either on or off the clock for every eight hour shift for anyone over the age of eighteen. It is up to the employers' discretion when or if these breaks are given.

- At least one half hour break, AND two fifteen minutes breaks off the clock is mandatory for every eight hour shift for anyone age of seventeen and under. It is up to the employer if these breaks are given or if the employer would rather face a fine.

Note that if the employee is over the age of eighteen, it is not required and is up to the "discretion of the employer" as to if, when and how much of a break they are allowed. It would seem that if the casinos could cut down on breaks by having an all non-smoking work force, then they could keep the same dealers at the tables for longer stretches. In turn, with less time changing dealers and more hands of blackjack played, you have an uninterrupted stream of players throwing money on the table (which we all know mostly goes to the house). Who needs a break? There are no clocks, no windows, hell; dealers aren't allowed to carry cell phones or wear wristwatches. Who cares, as long as the casino is making their money?

Hiring a non-smoker would ensure that this steady stream of cash hitting the table goes uninterrupted, even for a 30-second dealer shift. Studies have shown that when a dealer who has formed a rapport at his table, good or bad, packs up and walks away from the table, people's attention turn to the other games in the casino. This interrupts the game and the cash flow, and casinos try to avoid this lapse at all costs. A smoker that needs to leave the table every three hours to light up or take a drag breaks the chain of concentration, and it would seem that casinos would try to avoid this distraction any way possible; even to the point of refusing to hire nicotine addicts under the guise of "public health." Las Vegas casinos have come under fire for the same bullying tactics, to the point where they faced lawsuits from several dealers who have been denied bathroom breaks and are now experiencing kidney and bladder problems as the result of such long term denial of bodily functions.

Many non-smoking office workers feel it is "unfair" that all employees are given a fifteen minute smoke break. How is it unfair if the non-smoking employee is also given fifteen minutes to go "not" smoke if they wish? If you look at it from a strictly monetary point of view and you cut out breaks for just the black jack dealers, then you don't have to hire at least one or two full time or 3 to 4 part time people to cover those breaks. That in itself cuts out about 40 to 60 hours per week plus benefits, and this is *just* for the dealers. Now apply that formula to the entire casino staff. Wow!

This, of course, is only in reference to smokers. Users of snuff, snus, patches, gum, lozenges and even e-cigs are discreet in their use and require no "special" breaks in order to indulge their habit or addiction. That's where the "time is money" principle no longer applies and the casino industry claims another reason for not hiring nicotine users is that they get better rates on their insurance by having a tobacco-free workforce.

Casino Royale: An Insider's Perspective
By Bill Johnson

I've probably spent half my life in casinos. I've been to pretty much every remotely big name-casino in North America and Great Britain, and there's three things that will always be present in the most successful of gambling establishments-smoke, liquor and women.

Massachusetts and New York make a pretty hefty return from their smoke-free casinos. But compare them to Louisiana, Atlantic City or Las Vegas and you'll see how short they come up side-by-side with smoking casinos. In the world of professional gambling, there's really only two locations that anyone takes seriously: Las Vegas and Atlantic City.

When people go into a casino, they expect smoke. Even non-smokers, who have never taken a drag in their life, will smoke a free 40-dollar cigar if it's comped to them while they're being raped by the one-armed bandit. The entire atmosphere of a successful casino is enveloped in smoke and alcohol, with beautiful women serving them up in heaps.

But if you enter one of these new-fangled smokeless casinos, the free-wheeling decadence that Vegas tourists and Atlantic City rollers experience is gone. In turn, they feel more "responsible" and are apt to spend less. I don't care how many free Snapples you send my way, if I have to go outside to smoke a cigar, I'm not having fun and I'm just going to go to a different casino.

On the other hand, since the 70's, the casino guys got together and decided that their dealers and hostesses shouldn't be walking around with a cigarette on display. The reasoning was that the average player would look at the dealer as "just another guy like me" who could possibly deal a bad hand or something stupid, which didn't inspire confidence in that particular dealer. Pretty soon the fat stogie-chomping green-hats were replaced by young, good-looking men that acted like robots and dressed like bellboys. And you know what? It worked. The money kept pouring in, which is the only thing in the entire world a casino operator cares about. STE

This doesn't make sense if the employer pays X amount across the board for Y number of employees, then if an employee uses tobacco, he or she would have to cover the difference in the premium. When I am offered health care or life insurance premiums they always specify "nicotine user" and "NON-nicotine user." With no differentiation between snus, snuff, pipes, cigars, or cigarettes... other less harmful tobacco alternatives. In one fell swoop, all nicotine products have been uniformly damned, unless it comes from the big pharmaceutical companies (and in the case of the Ohio casinos, even those are verboten.) In reality, if they would just take the time to look at the numbers and read the studies, they would see just how wrong they are.

So now even our insurance companies have gotten into the racket. Up until a few years ago there were rates for "Smokers" and "NON-smokers," now it is "Tobacco users" and "NON-tobacco users." This now financially penalizes people like my husband who uses snus and snuff. Even though it is proven the pasteurization of Swedish snus and many snuff products are extremely less harmful than burning tobacco and that it could be a less harmful alternative to the big pharmaceutical companies' alternative drugs like Chantix (one side effect of which is suicide), these anti-tobacco-Nazis see any form of tobacco as bad, and is to be banned at all cost. To them tobacco equals nicotine, nicotine is an addictive drug, which is bad... unless it is "nicotine" from a pharmaceutical company in the form of a patch or gum, which has proven to be just as if not more dangerous, and much less effective at curbing addiction.

Alcohol is just as addictive for some as nicotine is for others, and we see how well banning it went. Although prohibition happened all at once, tobacco is being banned slowly over time. Setting a minimum mandatory purchase age was fair, but it didn't slow down the teenagers getting their hands on it. Then they raised the price, by raising the taxes slowly over time to the point that they thought no one could afford it. And yes, many did quit. But even more switched to cheaper alternatives like smokeless or black-market smokes. The campaign then switched to "Save the Children." Now that the children are safe, they are trying to save *me*. What part of, "Hey Mr. and Mrs. Anti-tobacco Nazi, I DON'T WANT TO BE SAVED!" do they not understand?

How far are we willing to allow these anti-tobacco screwheads to go before we start to stand up and say, "NO?" At what point do MY rights as a tobacco user matter? When are people going to notice just how downward a spiral we're on? Today it is nicotine, what will it be tomorrow? We live in a country formed under the idea that our personal rights are God-given and we are free to be an individual. Or at least I thought.

As I have said in many of my articles at Snuscentral.com, "I am an adult, and I don't need someone to choose what is right or wrong for me." I know that nicotine is a drug. I understand it is addictive. I have listened to all of the BS propaganda about tobacco use. The good, the bad, and the ugly... and I choose to use it. Anti-tobacco pundits have always generally used the statistics from cigarette smokers to "prove" their points regarding all tobacco use. Tobacco use and cigarette smoking are not interchangeable. Please stop lumping me, a six-pinch a day nasal snuffer, statistically into the same category as the guy that smokes three packs a day. Other than the fact that we are hated by a certain societal segment, we have no more in common than a communist and a capitalist.

Thank you Mr. and Mrs. Noseybody, but I don't need to be saved. I am a grown woman and my right to do to my body what I wish, whether it be to drink, smoke, eat or fornicate, concerns you naught. Long live tobacco and the rights of the people who choose to enjoy it!

STE

Post - Apocalyptic Snuff

By Nigel McCarren

Photography by Elisha Cozine

AS we all know, civilization ended on the 12th (or was it the 21st?) of December 2012. Those of us who ignored Nostradamus, David Icke, the New World Order folks and the rest are now smiling on the other side of our faces. Zombies roam the city centres, North American Grays continually abduct us and do unspeakable things with probes and the global Tsunami has ruined all of the tobacco crops. That bit really hurt. But, those of us spared at the Tribulation (nearly forgot that one) still need our Vitamin N; so we need to add snuff-making skills alongside defensive shooting (or defensive stick-waiving if you are in the UK), machete sharpening and beard growing. You are not a prepper if you are not wearing a big beard - c'mon, you *know* this, right? So let's get busy and make that N-powder.

First off, you need to source your tobacco and you want some that has already had a lot of the work done for you - this is no time to start sowing, growing and curing organic tobacco strains, maybe when we have re-claimed the land, but right now you need something to snuff, so let's use a proprietary roll your own tobacco. Get yourself kitted out in your body armour, strap that pump-action on (gun, I mean) and get down to your local store. The looters will have stripped the shelves pretty bare by now but with some perseverance you should be ok. I found myself 100g of Golden Virginia hand rolling tobacco. True, I had to beat someone's head in for it but that's a story for the next issue... if there is one of course.

STEP ONE: *There are two ways to go about procuring your tobacco: armed or unarmed. Guess which method ends in your death!*

Golden Virginia (GV) is a fine-cut blend of Virginia (obviously), Burley and Oriental; the three types that are the most common in cigarette tobaccos. There are a couple of immediate advantages in using a blend like this: the fine, shredded tobacco is very easy to reduce to powder when dried and it is an excellent vehicle for a wide variety of flavorings or sauces. It is a blend that will carry less of it's flavour through to the finished product, making it an ideal medium to experiment with. Of course you can use anything you like but if you use, say, broken up cigars or pipe tobacco then you will get a lot of that flavour in the finished snuff. Great if you want those tastes - and by all means use them - this is a magazine article, not martial law - but you will struggle to get a lighter tasting snuff out of them. You could make a fair approximation of an SP with GV, but with heavier, darker tobacco that would be hard because those citrus top-notes would just get swamped, and whilst you won't get a realistic SP out of a dark, robust tobacco you can, to an extent, make a rich, dark snuff out of GV. It's versatile.

Ok, you need to get the tobacco to the point where it is as dry as a bone (not one of yours though). A shredded tobacco like GV dries out very quickly and you want that to happen because it will help you to take it down to the snuff grade that you like - coarse, medium-coarse or fine. As any old roll-your-own infected undead-person knows, the leaf dries out in no time if it is not kept in an airtight container - bad news for smokers, good for those evading Zombie hordes who need to move from place to place every few days. Of course you could put the stuff in the oven for a couple of hours on a low heat and dry it out that way. Except there are no ovens left. So, get yourself any kind of container, dump the tobacco in there and cover with something that is porous enough to let the atmosphere in, but keep insects and the like out. Keep going back to it every once in a while to see how it is doing; you want it to be at the point that it literally turns to dust for a fine snuff, less so if you want it coarse. At total de-hydration it will more or less turn itself into a fine flour, and this is the best grade for this particular tobacco.

STEP TWO: *Whether you're male or female, team up with as many women as you can. Then train them to cover you while you're monkeying around with the snuff recipe. Don't forget to give them guns. And styling products.*

When the tobacco is at the desired moisture, you need to grind it. Drying a processed tobacco will always drive off some of the aromatics that give it it's character - so de-hydrating and then *re-hydrating* sounds illogical but the resulting dryness makes milling at home with simple tools much easier. You can use various types of coffee-mill (hand cranked for you, obviously), food processors or just an old fashioned mortar and pestle. A mortar and pestle can be easily improvised to make this small amount of snuff; a cereal bowl and glass spice jar would work well enough. Take the tobacco and grind it up in small amounts and you are then at the stage that I always love the most: flavouring. This is where you get to indulge your palate and your imagination, and what better way to take your mind off the lack of McDonald's and Starbucks?

There are numerous methods of flavouring tobacco and making snuff so this is really a bastardized version of one of the quicker methods, i.e make the flour and then add a sauce. In the long-lost ages of pre-2012, each snuff maker did things according to their own traditions, from flavouring (casing) the tobacco before it was milled, letting it age in barrels, this that and the other. This method gives you a snuffable product in quick-time.

The most direct, and easiest method, is to simply make your flavouring sauce, add it to the tobacco and let it mature - in effect, a snuff sauce is nothing more than a marinade. You could add dry ingredients - you could add anything you like - but it's better to get the flavour out of the ingredient and then add it. If you intend using liquor in your snuff consider de-naturing it a touch by boiling off some or all of the alcohol. Neat liquor can give a kind of raw taste to the snuff, something like a red-wine sauce that has not been properly cooked through. But, if you want that booze, go for it: there are no rules in taste.

If you want to go to town with straight liquor, like bourbon or cognac, and you are just making a small amount you could experiment with the evaporation method; this is simply placing the Jack D. or booze of choice in a shallow dish and setting it down next to, or in, the snuff in it's container. Works for small batches but anything over a few hundred grammes and it becomes a little impractical. If you wanted a bourbon flavoured snuff, and you wanted a large amount, direct addition would be best, maybe even a hybrid sauce of de-natured and straight up. These points are the things of great debate because everyone who makes snuff has their own opinions - experimentation is the key to making good home-made snuff and articles like this are just guides. Personally, I would ignore anyone that said 'this is the only way.' (Those types of people are the reason we're living a post-apocalyptic zombie nightmare, remember?)

When you have added the flavouring it is then a question of letting the snuff mature. The exact point at which it is ready is down to personal taste, just go back to it at whiles and see if you like it, simple as that. Commercially made snuffs have various things added to potentiate nicotine, enhance flavour, stabilize to avoid or stop fermentation etc etc - I would not go down that route with proprietary brands because in one way or another it has already been through the initial processing stage. I would let the snuff mature in an airtight vessel at room temperature - exactly what that is is not vitally important, neither is darkness or light with a small amount. This will be ready in a couple of weeks and there is not much to go wrong as long as it is in an airtight container. Mould is sometimes a threat to a batch of snuff but as the source tobacco is already very stable the conditions for mould growth are just not there unless you add them - use the same standards of hygiene as you would with preparing a meal and it will be fine. The local horde is howling outside my door so here's a very simple recipe:

Quick Post-Apocalyptic snuff recipe:

Ingredients:
100g of Golden Virginia RYO tobacco or similar, dried and milled.
Good quality port
Strong, good quality instant coffee of choice
A teaspoon, or to taste, of vanilla essence

Method

Take sufficient port to moisten the flour to the level you enjoy. Bring to the boil and simmer for 10 minutes and allow to cool. Add the coffee whilst warm enough to ensure it dissolves fully. Add the vanilla essence. Combine with the flour, adding sufficient to moisten to the desired level. Place in a clean, odorless vessel and leave for one to two weeks.

Pack in your bug-out bag to provide emergency snuff-cover on your next foraging mission. Enjoy as required and obviously the ingredients, ratios and what have you can be altered to taste. 100g gives you a worthwhile amount of snuff. Enough to use for a few days while whittling away at the walking dead population encroaching your territory.

Nigel McCarren *is the snuff blender behind the mind-blowing Abraxas brands and is the former owner/operator of the Snuffhouse forums. You can purchase any of Nigel's products through Mr. Snuff, the internet's largest snuff emporium.*

Elisha Cozine *is a professional photographer based out of Fayetteville, NC and enjoys photographing beautiful young women running away from some unseen Lovecraftian terror. She also does family portraits and is great with kids! See her studio's ad in this month's issue for booking information.*

Be Prepared.

STOCK UP ON ALL OF YOUR FAVORITE SNUFFS (INCLUDING ABRAXAS, CERISE AND DRAGUN) BY ORDERING FROM MISTERSNUFF.COM. DO IT *BEFORE* THE ZOMBIES COME...

The Finer Points
With Mr. Manners

Your Guide to the Proper Etiquette and Refined Mannerisms Whilst Partaking of Snuff.

As Dictated to Seth Desjardins

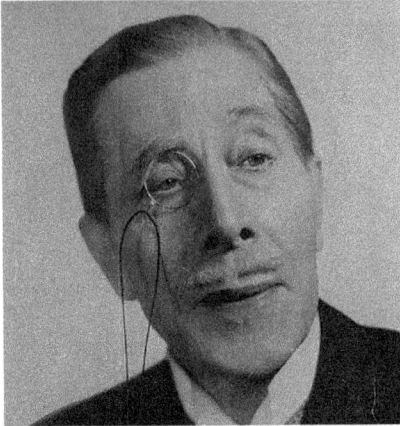

Greetings once again fellow snuff enthusiasts! I was so delighted when my assistant informed me that I had been asked to once again enlighten you upon the virtues and valor of snuff taking here in the pages of the Snuff Taker's Ephemeris that I immediately went to my secret chambers to unearth the legendary Wilson's Ghost Snuff! Undoubtedly, this snuff has been decanted in the jeweled skull of a Nordic tribesman, the last of his tribe, in fact; as this is the fashion of the sophisticated gentleman. I only partake in the consumption of Ghost Snuff on the most special of occasions and this is one of them! Naturally you are unfamiliar with Wilson's Ghost Snuff because it is the most exclusive snuff on earth and available to only those who extol the utmost adherence to snuff taking propriety. Ghost Snuff is so finely ground that it is imperceptible to the naked eye! Of course only the most experienced, adept and refined snuff takers can even conceptualize such an exquisite grind of tobacco. I am unsurprised, yet still very pleased indeed, that a man of manners and stature of the late 19th and early 20th Century is having such an immense impact on those interested in the finer points of snuff taking here in the 21st Century! I shall delay no longer and proceed to answer your queries with utmost precision and accuracy!*

*Editors note:

Mr. Manners was tragically lost on an expedition to harvest walrus tusks in northern Greenland in 1926. While the rest of his crew lost their lives, Mr. Manners used his wit and guile to place himself in the frozen waters of the Arctic Ocean; freezing and preserving himself intact to be reanimated in the future. The future is now!

Dear Mr. Manners,

With the first use of nasal snuff occurring on the Iberian Peninsula and the first snuff mill having been established in Spain, what impact do you think this has upon snuff culture? And what do you make of the theory that "SP" is an abbreviation for Spanish therefore meaning SP's are influenced by Spanish snuff?

Sincerely,

Julian Howard
Eye, Suffolk, UK

Do you have tiny eyes good fellow? I've heard men from Eye, Suffolk are afflicted with tiny eyes, sir. Along with your tiny eyes, it seems you have a tiny intellect, sir. The myth that snuff was first produced in Spain is pure Catholic propaganda to diminish the stature of hard working and innovative Protestants. It is the Catholic Church I tell you that has perpetrated this lie as they try to subvert history in order to diminish the Protestant contribution to society. Let me ask you sir, when was nasal snuff first thought to be used? The early 1500's. And when did the Protestant Church come to be, sir? The year 1500, sir. Coincidence? I think not! Could one then say that nasal snuff was God's gift to the people for the formation of the Protestant Church, sir? One could, I believe, sir.

As for your second question, SP certainly does not stand as an abbreviation for "Spanish," all men of manner and stature know that SP stands for "Sheffield's Pride!"

Mr. Manners,

How do you rate American Scotch Snuffs in comparison to High Dry Toasts?

Junior McCoy Sr.
Knob Lick, Kentucky, USA

Allow me to ruminate on your name for a moment. Your first name is Junior, yet the suffix with which you present yourself makes it clear you are in fact the first with this name. Your father was not named Junior because you are a Sr. and I have extrapolated that your son is Junior McCoy Jr. Your name, my good man, is as perplexing as a Kafka novel. Sir, it is clear that you are not the result of selective breeding. Whilst this puts you at a great disadvantage as you work your way towards the ladder of sophistication and stature, it is my hope that my guidance will at least give you the glimmer of hope that you will one day be a true gentleman.

Until your question came across my fine ebony and mahogany desk, I had never heard of Scotch Snuff. Undeterred, I asked my assistant to retrieve his shoddy snuff collection and present to me a variety of such snuffs to sample. I first tried the meretriciously named "Rooster." My assistant informs me that many an American snuff taker enjoys this and to them I say, "Phooey!" This "snuff" smells of burnt wood and evokes thoughts of banjos, decrepit dirt farms and other unpalatable aspects of American "culture." I moved on next to try "Top's Mild." This has a more subtle flavoring of burning wood, but continues to be a one dimensional snuff at best. I then tried "Honest" snuff and I can tell you my good man, there is nothing honest about this snuff whatsoever.

At this point in my sampling, I had to contact my personal physician to perform a procedure on my nose in order to get my sense of smell back. Never in all my years had such a vicious assault on my olfactory senses occurred, and I was gassed by the Huns in the Great War!

With the constitution and conviction only befitting a man of stature and status like myself, I persevered undeterred through the last two Scotch "snuffs." I would like to note that I did this for you, the reader, so that I may impart upon you the means and manners to assist you in becoming a most elegant snuff taker. But I digress; I ordered my assistant to get me a snifter of brandy and then tried the peculiarly named "Dental" Scotch. I did not find this snuff to differentiate itself significantly from the "Honest" snuff, but I can say that for unknown reasons I tolerated it better than the previously smelled varieties. Finally, I sampled "Standard." I am not sure if the name implies that it is the standard bearer of snuffs or if it is simply a standard variety. I can say with certainty that neither is the case. With that said, I found it to have similarities to the "Rooster," but without the off-putting burnt wood scent. I stop short of saying any of these "snuffs" are enjoyable and I sincerely doubt I will try them again. It would be unfitting for any man of manner and virtue to indulge in such a snuff. With that said, and at the risk of alienating myself from my constituency, there are elements particularly with the "Standard" and "Dental" varieties that I could count as admirable (if I were a downtrodden American dweller of the hills.)

Since I have been long-winded in my assessment of these American Scotch "snuffs" I will end with some brevity. My High Dry Toast of choice is the Fribourg & Treyer recipe. With that said there are many other fine toasts available; Fribourg & Treyer High Dry Toast is simply my preference. A preference you should heed however because, after all, I am the authority on mannerisms befitting the refined man of today. I can understand how you may make a parallel between these American Scotches and an authentic High Dry Toast, but I can tell you, Mr. Junior Sr., that the offerings from America do not offer the complexity, subtlety and enjoyability found in a High Dry Toast. Not only that, but a man of status would never think to have such an unrefined snuff in his snuffbox.

Mr. Manners,

In the last issue of the *Snuff Taker's Ephemeris*, you claimed that there was no such thing as French snuff, yet anyone who knows anything about the history of tobacco knows that Jean Nicot de Villemaine introduced snuff to France in 1561 as a gift to the mother of King François II, Catherine de Medici as a cure to the king's headaches. Naturally this means that there is in fact French snuff and France has a large role in the proliferation of snuff throughout Europe and eventually the world. What say you?

Ancel Rousseau
Condoum, France

French snuff?! FRENCH SNUFF!? Poppycock! Pure, unadulterated poppycock! Is it not bad enough that my able, yet morally deficient assistant is partly of French descent?! The very fact that I have to work each day knowing that my assistant is a cowardly, unhygienic, untrustworthy Frenchman is enough to send one into fits of delirium!Can you imagine working day after day knowing that, although speaking the Queen's English quite well, your assistant cannot shed the binds of his genes and truly walk into the light of sophistication and stature? Lucky for me, he is subdued with plenty of blended Scotch, fine English ales and loose women. Not only do I have to live in fear that my assistant of French ancestry may one day reveal his genetic disposition and stab me in the heart for a baguette, I have to answer a challenge from a Frenchman?! It is fortunate that a man of my status and composure has dedicated himself to refining snuff takers and dispelling myths so that all may have an opportunity to step out of the darkness and into the light!

"...There are elements, particularly with the "Standard" and "Dental" varieties, that I could count as admirable (if I were a downtrodden American dweller of the hills)..."

How Did You Know I Use Dental Sweet Snuff?"
Because the Sweetest Girl in the World . . . .
Should Use the Best Sweet Snuff in the World!"

If you will take off your beret, put down your 9th glass of substandard wine, your horrendous cheese and your stale bread I will enlighten you to the true origins of snuff. Snuff was invented by, and I hesitate to say this, an Irishman. Luckily for him he moved to England at an early age. It is true that the damned Spaniards and Portuguese were the first to bring to tobacco to Europe from the Western Hemisphere, but the truth is they were too unrefined to know what to do with it. Like the savages they are, they decided that smoking tobacco, like the tribes of the Western Hemisphere, was the best way to take tobacco.

The aforementioned Irishman, Nicolas O'Teene- after being brought into the light of English society, was the first person to grind tobacco into snuff. This is common knowledge for any man of status and I am unsurprised that you would subscribe to the centuries old propaganda that permeates the history books.

STE

Have a question for Mr. Manners? Contact his assistant @ seth@apandpcomics.com or tweet at him @SethDesjardins - that is, so long as you're not a stinky Frenchman.

Mr. Manners' viewpoints do not necessarily reflect those of his assistant or the staff of the Snuff Taker's Ephemeris. *On the other hand, we agree with him much of the time, so whatevs.*

The Most Expensive Snuff in the World Part II

A Special Fang-in-Cheek Ephemeris Travelogue by

Beck Linden

"This is the threshing floor," Lillith said. We were standing on a staircase approximately 30 feet in the air. Below us, the bare concrete floors echoed with the sound of machinery and men. About ten malnourished-looking males in their late fifties pushed buttons and pulled levers, cursing in their own language. Some fed raw tobacco leaves into one end of an enormous steel tube. At the other end, finely ground particles were collected by a worker holding a rusty bucket. As the snuff would just about reach the lid, another man would walk up with an empty bucket and collect the now-full container from the first man.

"This is actually pretty cool," I said. "Where do you add the flavorings?"

"Flavorings?" she asked. "We use no flavorings. Carpathian tobacco is the finest on earth and needs no such adulteration."

"So... You basically pour the buckets into smaller consumer tins and that's that?"

Lillith didn't answer immediately. "Let me show you the second part of the manufacturing process."

We walked back down the corridor that we originally entered through. I saw Greta and the nameless one standing at the end of one hall, evil-eyeing me as if I was sleeping with their husbands (or wives). We turned a corner and stepped into a modern, carpeted office. Soft music played lightly in the background. A wooden desk sat in the corner, opposite a closet door. It was padlocked shut.

"When you asked me about flavorings," Lillith said, "I wasn't entirely truthful. We do add one extra ingredient to Uskat Krut that makes it the most desired of all snuff brands. This vital... ingredient... is so rare that it takes us many months to make even one batch of snuff." She pulled a key out of her bustier and slid it into the padlock. "Nobody from the outside knows what this ingredient is. Nobody that isn't one of us." The lock clicked and she removed it from the latch. She turned the knob and swung the door wide open.

What I saw almost made me vomit. There on the floor sat a bound and gagged young girl, no older than 16 by her looks. Tears, grime and blood stained her face. Her wild eyes pleaded with mine for help. Instinctively I reached down to help her to her feet, and Lillith knocked me backwards with a swipe of her hand.

"What the f..." I began, before Lillith grabbed my mouth and clamped it shut. "No questions," she said. "Just listen." The girl whimpered and sobbed as I stood there in shock. "This girl was a peasant... an orphan. She came to us willingly, knowing fully who we are and what we do. She pledged herself to us, in exchange for being allowed to live in luxury for a short time. For two years she has enjoyed hot showers, warm meals and internet chatrooms. But now the time has come for the lamb to be slaughtered, and the bitch cries like a lost dog."

A Journey to Carpathian Ruthenia in search of Uskat Krüt

"I'm still not understanding…" I said. "You're going to kill her, but for what?"

"For her blood," came a response from the back of the room. It was Greta. "Our snuff is mixed with the blood of peasant virgins. The blood is married to the tobacco in a most exquisite manner, where it ferments for six months before being sold for the top dollar. Every vampire in Europe knows of its existence. Few mortals have ever heard of it, and we do our best to pretend it is only a legend. A myth, started by fools and retold by tourists."

"So does it really knock your socks off, like the guys at *The Ephemeris* said it did?" I was actually getting curious now, which made me feel guilty, what with all the crying and whimpering in the background.

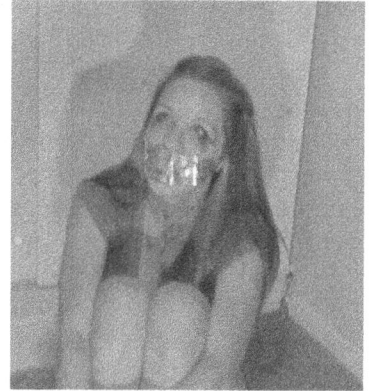

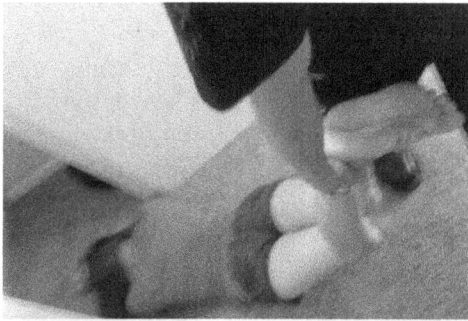

"When a mortal experiences our snuff, he is lucky if his heart does not explode. Such is the potency of the blood. For two years, this girl has been on a steady diet of special herbs and tinctures that awaken the pleasure receptors in our brains. Human beings have no such neurons, and so the pleasure turns into an overwhelming experience that the body processes as shock. Think of it as heroin or morphine; an experienced junkie regularly injects doses that would kill a first time user."

She went on. "Even in a container, the snuff must be kept out of natural sunlight, for it will disintegrate and melt, much like our Hollywood counterparts do in the last five minutes of the horror film." I thought back to the incident in the taxi, where the chalice of Uskat Krut melted a hole through the floorboard. "For your three man-friends to still be alive and to crave more of this most special of snuffs, they must have a very high tolerance for tobacco."

"Yeah, Rob actually injects nicotine into his veins like it was dope. Mick and Micah give each other tobacco enemas until they hallucinate. They're pretty hardcore dudes." For once, Lillith seemed impressed.

"Now, you shall see how we extract the ingredient." With a sharp whistle, two pale but masculine boy-men entered the room. One grabbed the girl's arms while the other held her by her legs. Together they raised her and carried her off to another room. As they were carting her into the hall, her hands broke loose and grabbed the edge of the doorway. Her legs were thrashing like an animal. One of the men slapped her in the face and she let go of the doorjamb.

Lillith turned around and motioned to Greta. "Call in Victoria." Greta nodded and disappeared down the hall.

"Who's Victoria?" I asked, wondering if I really wanted to even know.

"Victoria is our master blender," Lillith sighed, as if she tired of my questioning. "She extracts the ingredients. You'll like her a great deal. She has a way of making even the most routine of procedures feel like a grandiose party."

I followed Lillith as we walked into another office. The peasant girl was now tied down to a wooden desk, her head teetering off the edge and her eyes darting about wildly. A tall, gorgeous blonde with black rimmed glasses walked into the room. "Oooooh," she cooed in a thick German accent, "Ve haf wisitors." She extended her hand to mine, and for reasons unknown, I kissed it. "So polite! I am Wictoria. You are in for real treat."

Lillith circled the girl, touching her body softly, whispering words of comfort in the girl's native language. She seemed to have calmed down somewhat. Victoria began kissing the girl gently on the neck, moving slowly down to her bellybutton. One of the men pulled a black cloth bag over the girl's face and tied it tightly across her neck. Then, with a blinding speed, Victoria's canine teeth extended downward 3/4ths of an inch and before my mind could process it, her face was buried in the girl's stomach.

The peasant girl screamed inside the hushed confines, the only other sound being Vicoria's gnashing and chewing. After a few seconds, her head lifted and I could see what looked like part of the girl's liver hanging over her bottom lip. Victoria made a loud *ummmm* sound, like a man who just bit into the best piece of Thanksgiving turkey he's ever tasted. "Yes," she whispered breathlessly, "this one is ready."

With a quick snap of the wrist, Lillith tore the cover off of the girl's head and laughed maniacally into her face. I could see that Lillith's fangs were also poking out, like two pieces of white picket fence, glistening with saliva. I was starting to feel nauseous now, and I looked around the room for something to puke in. One of the men grabbed me from behind while the other held open the black bag that had been tied around the victim's head. I violently retched and dry-heaved for a couple of minutes, as I had nothing in my belly to actually vomit up.

When I was able to stop heaving, I rubbed the water out of my eyes and watched Lillith as she sucked freely from the girl's neck. Lillith's hands were covered in blood and a cruel, broad smile filled her face in between sucks.

Greta walked over with a white funnel and handed it to Lillith. "Where is she?" Lillith snarled, just as the nameless one entered the room with a large black bucket. "I am here, my mistress." Lillith snatched the bucket out of her hand and slapped her hard on her bottom. "Go now, whore."

The funnel was held to the girl's neck and a torrent of blood gushed through it and into the bucket. After what seemed an eternity, the bucket was nearly full and I could see that all signs of life had vanished from the peasant girl's eyes. As Lillith walked away with the bucket, the others in the room swooped in on the corpse like vultures, each tearing and ripping at her body in search of whatever leftover blood still remained in her carcass.

Lillith handed the bucket over to one of the men. "Send this to the threshing floor," she said. Pointing at me, she beckoned with her finger. "Follow me." Down the hall we walked until we reached what so far had turned out to be the largest of offices. A huge cherrywood desk filled the room. Atop it sat a computer monitor, phones and fax lines. A large photocopier sat in the background. Had I not just witnessed the carnage in the other room, I could have believed I was in my editor's office back in New York. A portrait of Vlad Tepest, hung over the comfy-looking leather chair, helped to remind me that I was knee deep in vampire territory. Lillith sat down in the leather chair and motioned for me to have a seat in one of the less-padded vinyl lounge chairs.

"What," she asked, "do you think of what you have just witnessed?" I struggled to find the right words to say.

"I'm not really sure," I honestly answered. "I just saw a girl die. It made me sick. But at the same time I felt no pity for her." Lillith's eyes gleamed as I said this. "I was actually kind of excited to see the blood flow, and really, I was kind of sad that it ended so quickly." Lillith crossed her fingers together and folded her palms.

"This is all true, then?" she said, looking into my eyes for any hint of deception.

"I swear."

Lillith whistled again and within seconds, the entire group had taken position inside her office. The men flanked her on either side, while the women kneeled on the ground next to her. Another man entered the office carrying a glass plate full of dark powder, the same hue as paprika. He carefully placed it on her desk and walked away backwards, his eyes never once leaving Lillith's until he was far enough down the hallway.

"This," Lillith said, sweeping her hand over the plate, "is what remains of our last batch." She pulled out a

letter opener from within the desk drawer and began cutting the snuff into long, thin rails. Victoria was the first to bend over and snuff a line. She leaned back into Lillith's lap just as Lillith began to slink to the floor. She snuffed three lines altogether, each one producing what can only be described as a massive orgasm. She pinched a small quantity between her thumb and forefinger and tossed it onto the ground, where Greta began to lap it up like a dog. She reached behind her and grabbed Victoria's leg, propping it up on the desk. Lillith put two small mounds of the snuff on Victoria's upper thigh and motioned for the men to take their fill. Eagerly, they snuffed the powder up and licked the spot where the snuff was originally placed. Then they returned to their previous stance, backs to the wall, eyes staring at nothing.

I was so eager to try it, yet scared to death at the same time. Lillith must have sensed this, for she scraped a small portion off of the plate and on to the desk before whistling for the manservant to come back and retrieve it.

"As I have warned you," she said, "this may very well end your life. But the temptation is too great, is it not? You must have what you should not have. The... forbidden fruit, I believe is the saying?" Eagerly I nodded. "Then this, my love, you shall try."

I leaned over the desk and separated the already-small mound of snuff into two smaller sections about the size of a pea. "Here goes everything," I said, as I snuffed the tiny bump of reddish-brown blood tobacco. It hit my brain almost immediately, like a baseball shot from a cannon. I felt a quick sense of intense euphoria, followed by my neck and back starting to melt into my chair. The sounds around me and the colors in my eyes drained away into a small corner and all was black. I was unconscious.

****

When I came to, I was lying on the bank of the river where I had initially started my journey. Somehow, I had left the castle/factory, gone on a day-long boat ride, and ended up sleeping in the mud with no panties on. *No panties on!* It hit me. *Good lord, I've been graped!* I thanked God for my short term memory loss.

I made my way back to town and found a taxi. I had no money, just the digital camera that I had carried with me during my trip. I pulled the SD card out and traded it to the cab driver for a trip back to the airport. Within three days I was back in the United States, hiding out in my apartment. I wasn't really sure why I was hiding, but I didn't want to speak to anyone, especially the guys from the magazine.

About a week went by and I finally garnered enough courage to answer the phone. It was Micah. He wanted to know what I found out about the snuff. He rattled off questions like a machine gun until I couldn't take it anymore.

"Stop! Calm the heck down!" He shut up. "Yes, I went to Europe. Yes, I checked around for you. No, I couldn't turn up anything." A long sigh came back from the other end. "Are you satisfied now?" He muttered something about women being useless and slammed the phone down into the receiver.

I knew that if I was to ever share what I knew about Uskat Krut with anyone, I would be dead in a matter of days. Plus, I was an accessory (or at least, an eyewitness) to a murder. I didn't want to have to explain myself to law enforcement. And who was going to believe any of it anyway? Bunch of lesbian vampires in Eastern Europe killing street girls and draining their blood in order to mix it with snuff. Yeah, sounds like a plausible story. I turned on a pot of coffee and sat back with the newspaper. The lurid headline grabbed at me from the front page: WOMAN FOUND IN ALLEY WITH THROAT CUT. Blah blah blah.

It was dusk. I hadn't been sleeping well since I returned home. I would pass out during the day and wake up about five in the afternoon. Even with sunglasses, it was just too frigging bright outside. Besides, I liked the night anyway. It gave me more time to accomplish what I needed to do.

I sipped my wine and waited until I saw Pat Sajak on my TV screen. It would be dark now. Time to go to work. I dressed skimpily and exited through the fire escape. I reached the street and hit the closest lesbian bar I could find. My eyes scanned the dive until I found my target. She would be perfect. She was big; a heavyset woman with a butch haircut and an ugly face. Probably a regular. Probably unliked.

I cozied up to her at the pool table and we shot the breeze for about ten minutes. I could tell that she was surprised that a woman of my beauty would even have the time of day for her. The more we talked, the less she embraced the Man role she had been acting for so long and began to sound more and more like a human. A woman. Finally, I had to make the proposition.

"Listen," I girlishly cooed, "I'm not the type of person to ask this, EVER, but... you want to go outside with me?" I motioned to the Exit door on the side of the bar, the one that led out into the alley. Before she could answer, I grabbed her hand and she followed me into the cool night. I kissed her passionately, and she returned the favor, her fat arms squeezing me tightly. They squeezed even tighter as I sunk my fangs into her jugular and severed her aorta. I caught the fountain of blood in my mouth as it sprayed into my face and my hair. For ten minutes I sucked the bitch dry, until nothing would come out. I shoved her limp, lifeless body into a stack of trashcans and walked away, satiated for another day or two.

I made sure to cover my face as I walked back to my apartment. Back up the fire escape and into my warm bed, I licked the last of the sanguine fluid from my fingertips and fumbled in my purse. I pulled out my silver Patrick Collins snuffbox and tapped out a respectable amount of Uskat Krut onto the back of my hand. I inhaled it feverishly, knowing that I deserved every last crumb of comfort. Finally satisfied in every way, I rolled over and slept the deep, guiltless sleep of an unrepentant sinner.

STE

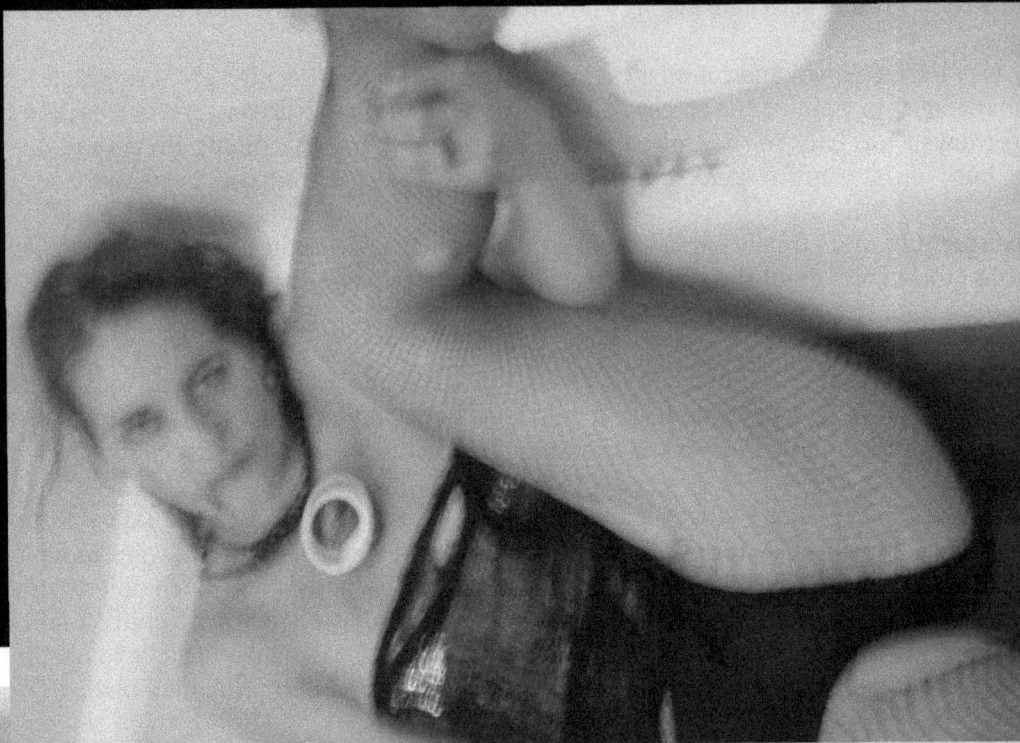

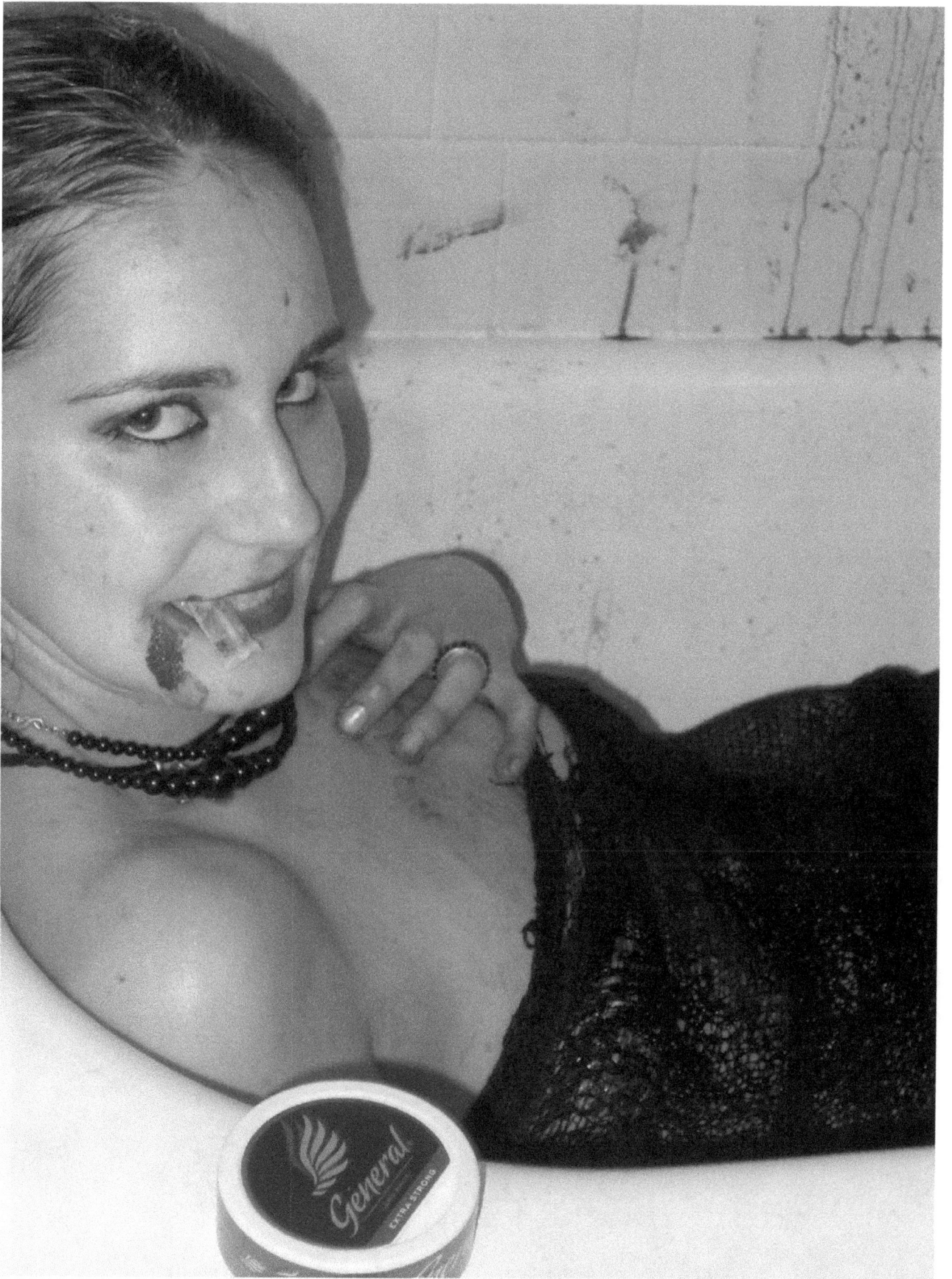

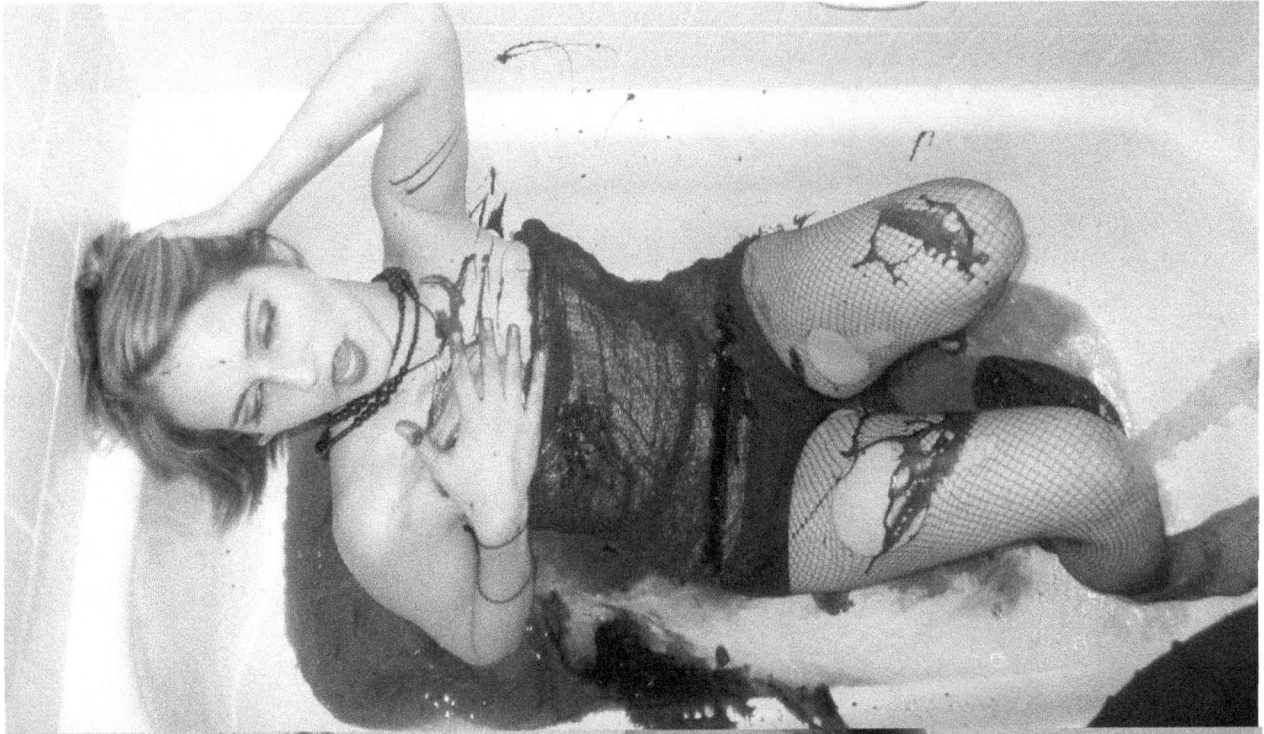

Offer One: Free Shipping and 50% off a Digital Subscription! Save 26.00!

One Year Print Subscription (Volumes 8, 9, 10 & 11) for 43.96 + **FREE SHIPPING** and a Year's Subscription (Vols 8-11) to our Digital E-zine for 9.99- **50% off!**

Total = 53.95!

(Free shipping good only for US & Canadian customers. All other customers please add $29.90 to cover shipping)

☐ Enclosed is a check or money order payable in US funds for 53.95. (US Customers only).

☐ Enclosed is a check or money order payable in US funds for 83.85. (Foreign orders only).

Offer Two: Free Shipping on our Print Edition! Save 16.00!

One Year Print Subscription (Volumes 8, 9, 10 & 11) for 43.96 + **FREE SHIPPING**

Total = 43.96!

(Free shipping good only for US & Canadian customers. All other customers please add $29.90 to cover shipping)

☐ Enclosed is a check or money order payable in US funds for 43.96. (US Customers only).

☐ Enclosed is a check or money order payable in US funds for 73.86. (Foreign orders only).

Offer Three: Subscribe to our E-zine and save 60% off the cover price of our print edition!

One Year Digital Subscription (Volumes 8, 9, 10 & 11) for 19.99 + FREE SHIPPING Save 23.97 off the cost of our print edition!

Total = 19.99! Full resolution .pdf copy delivered straight to your email box!

☐ Enclosed is a check or money order payable in US funds for 19.99.

MR. SNUFF Presents: The Connoisseur's Corner

Ever since our first issue, we've attempted to feature a review section that, for various reasons, just never materialized. When Dave from Mr. Snuff offered to pen just such an article, we couldn't say no!

*Note the title of this feature; The **Connoisseur's** Corner. This is a spotlight for snuffs that have shown an outstanding, consistent five-star rating from impartial costumers who liked the product so much that they took time out of their day to write an unpaid, unbiased review of said snuff. What better way to kick off this inaugural edition than with Abraxas, a brand which is on virtually all of the STE staff member's "Top 5" lists.*

By Clark Davis:

This snuff is top shelf. You can tell right away when you crack the seal and inhale the crafted aroma. I knew it was proper when I caught my wife, who abhors my snuff hobby, sneaking little whiffs of this blend. There is a spiciness and a sweetness present. There is a unique coffee nuance as well. There is a mature quality about this snuff. I live in remote Alaska, and have found the brisk Alaskan air invigorates the scent of Premium Batch Fin. I hope to try the original when it's available. Nice work and worth the price.

Rating: 5/5

By Erik Servia:

Another fine blend is about to hit the streets from Abraxas. I had the privilege of tasting Abraxas Premium Fin, which exceeded all expectations and should be described as nothing less than a spiritual experience. It is a snuff beyond comparison and one that I would be afraid to take as an all-day snuff at risk of losing the special feeling it gives me.

Abraxas Premium Fin screams class and luxury. Dark in color, the grind is fine and moist. Perfect to my liking and feels like snuffing pure silk. The flavor is incredibly rich and complex, with notes of fine liquors and premium blend coffee. But as it sits in the nose, I'm hit by something more-- A wonderfully decadent aroma like dark chocolate and fresh raspberries. All coming together like a very expensive, rich dessert in a five star restaurant. This snuff makes me want to buy a tuxedo and host lavish cocktail parties.

The flavor is quite lasting, but the taste of quality tobacco really shines towards the end. It also seems to be pretty generous in the Nic department, as I'm getting a bit light headed while typing this. It would be difficult for anyone to dispute the quality and craftsmanship of this blend, and it is one that you will not want to miss.

Rating: 5/5

By Jordan Beaulieu:

In the mood for something that is a step above your average snuff? How about a giant leap? You've found it! Dark, deep, exotic, intoxicating, rich. Meer adjectives seem unworthy when used to describe such a luxurious, omnipotent creation. Deep dark brown, pleasantly moist and coarse, it sits in your nose like a king on a throne - with authority. It has hints of the best arabic coffee and top shelf liquor, not the cheap stuff, but the stuff you buy only for special occassions. To compare this to your "run-of-the-mill" snuff is like trying to compare a Shelby GT500 to a 1980's Mustang with a 4 cylinder engine. Its like trying to compare your Grandma's home-made apple pie to the mass-produced imposter you bought at the corner store for 50 cents. There is no comparison, this is THE snuff, created with the delicate hands (and nose) of a master snuff maker. Not to be taken lightly, but to be savored and pondered upon by only the most serious of connoisseurs.

Rating: 5/5

By James Witteveen:

Our sense of smell opens up a world of feelings, sensations, and emotions. A certain odour can spark memories, stir up the imagination, and send you on a journey through time and space, transporting you to other worlds.

Abraxas provides just such an experience. An exquisitely flavoured snuff, created with passion and care by a skilled master who truly loves his craft, Abraxas is a vehicle that will take you on a journey to exotic climes and olden times, to places where senses are heightened, where sound, smell, taste, and sight are united in offering all that this world can give.

A good snuff can give you pleasure. A truly great snuff is pleasure in itself. Abraxas is a truly great snuff.

Rating: 5/5

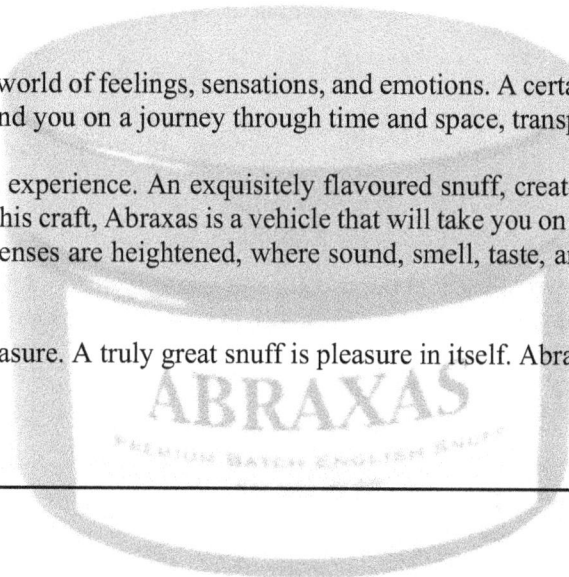

By M P McConnell:

This snuff is one product that lives up to its billing. The most noticeable characteristic of this snuff for me is its cigar leaf base, which is superb. My nose isn't as discerning as those of some other reviewers, but to me the tobacco base in this stuff is redolent of the finest Cuban cigar leaf; it has that distinctive taste. If this product does not in fact contain Cuban leaf, it is another feather in the cap of the blender; he knows his stuff.

On top of the cigar leaf base, the first thing one notices after smelling the jar is a fragrant cognac or other liqueur. The base and liqueur flavoring work in concert to produce the best snuff I have ever used. The flavoring lingers, but never overpowers.

As others have noted, the base is coarsely ground, dark, moist, and easily snuffed. This snuff will likely be appreciated most by snuffers who are fans of F&T products. The only respect in which the Abraxas does not compare favorably to the F&T line is in the nicotine content. The nicotine is there, but is not as high as the F&T products. This is a minor quibble, as it provides the perfect excuse to take more.

Highly recommended.

Rating: 5/5

By Robert Owen:

what can I say that hasn't been said? This snuff is worth the price. Clearly the Brandy and Port are all super high quality. The tobacco is out of this world. I wonder why there aren't more premium snuffs on the market. Every other tobacco product has variations in the level of quality and opulence. Finally snuff does again, too. Do yourself the favor and try this snuff. It's in my opinion the best snuff on the market. It hits all the bases. If you've ever smoked a decent cigar and a great cigar, that will tell you the level of difference between this snuff and others.

Rating: 5/5

By Paul Arntsen:

Excellent snuff! Opening the container, you are hit with a strong, fruity liqueur smell. At this point you can tell this is a premium snuff. It is rich, dark brown, coarse, moist fresh snuff, but not as coarse as some of the German snuffs. Once snuffed, the liqueur and tobacco linger in your nose for a long time. It is more of a refined flavor than F&T's, but that is the closest comparison. Just taking the lid off and smelling it is an awesome experience in itself!

I could use this all day but I prefer to use it in the evenings when I can enjoy all it has to offer (like a good Cuban cigar). I just hope more flavors of this quality are made in the future. Although the price is expensive, just remember the adage: "You get what you pay for."

Rating: 5/5

ABRAXAS

PREMIUM BATCH ENGLISH SNUFF

ab actu ad posse valet illatio

Warning: This product is not a safe alternative to cigarettes.

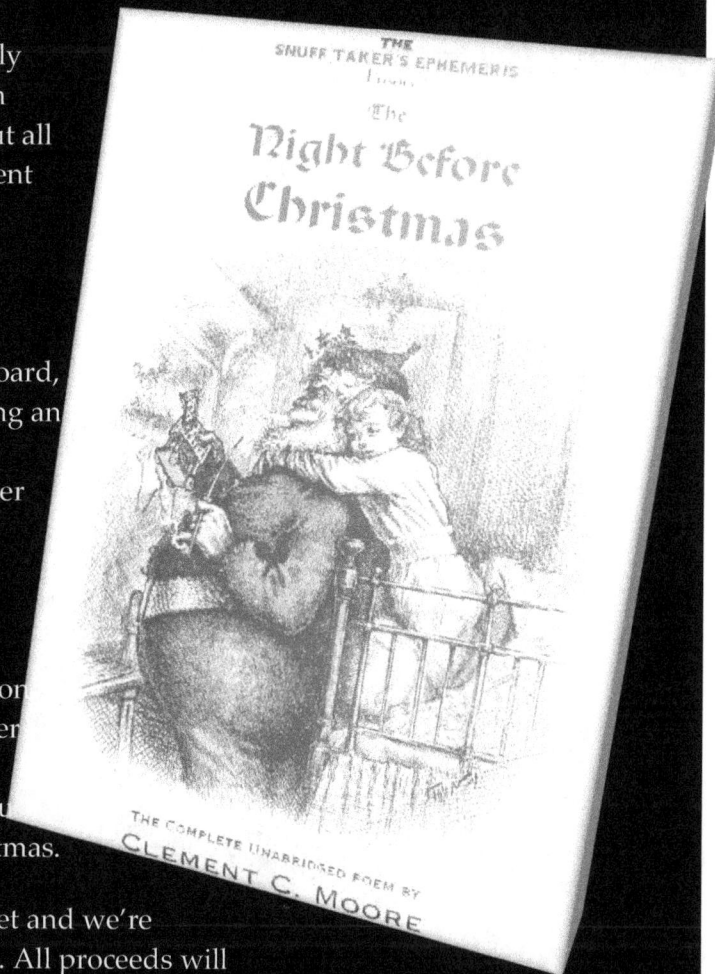

By
Simon
Handelsman

The Snuff Box

AND NOW, A WORD FROM OUR SPONSORS...

Advertising was always a part of trade. Both wholesalers and retailers advertised their wares in newspapers, city directories and almanacs. But, a better way to reach tobacco customers was to tell your business story on the cover of a snuff box. Often these advertising boxes were used as a premium or as a container given with the purchase of snuff.

The largest advertising snuff box produced may be this 5.5 inch box from Gail & Ax. Too expensive to be given away to customers, it likely sat on the tobacconist's counter to dispense a pinch of their snuff. The company started in 1860 and had up to 350 employees working in their factory on Barre Street in Baltimore making snuff and both chewing and smoking tobacco. They became part of the American Tobacco Company in 1891. Also, they believed in print advertising and are better known to collectors today for their trade cards and posters.

Many advertising boxes outline an inventory of the goods the proprietor carried often detailing the large assortment of flavors. Most of these snuff blends were originally compounded in the 18th century but continued to be popular in the 1900s. Another element that makes these advertising boxes instructive is the street and city address that usually appears. This allows the collector to research the firm and determine the date of the box.

 Typical specimens are the two round boxes above. The two manufacturers are both described as "Celebrated" and are located on the Front Street in New York City. The box on the left has a circular illustration at the center depicting an Indian with a bow in one hand and three tobacco leaves in the other. There is a ship under full sail in the background and a hogshead of tobacco.

The box has a circular legend proclaiming: "JAMES J. MAPES' CELEBRATED SNUFF AND TOBACCO MANUFACTORY." The small type tells the keen eyed:

"Where he has constantly on hand for sale, a large assortment of every article in his line, vix. Rosescent Macaboy, Scented, Plain & French coarse Rapee, American Gentleman, Princes Mixture, Demigros, Copenhagen, Maltese, Prince of Wales Mixture, Lancaster, Lundyfoots' Irish blackguard, Hardmans, Curracoa, Strasburgh, Violet, Nachitoches, Liberty Cap, Scotch and Roanoke Snuffs - Fine cut for chewing, Sweetscent chewing, American & Spanish smoking & Cavendish Tabaccos. SEGARS OF ALL QUALITIES. All the above Articles are warranted equal to any manufactured in the United States. Should they not be approved they can be returned and the money with the expenses will be refunded. P.S. Orders from any part of the Union will meet with prompt attentions."

The box on the right reads: "HENRY RIELL & CO's CELEBRATED SNUFF and TOBACCO MANUFACTORY" This box features a topless Indian maiden with the phrase "Trying is the Naked Truth." The hogshead is labeled Best Virginia. The copy features: "SPANISH, NEW ORLEANS, KITEFOOT AND AMERICAN SEGARS as well as SNUFF AND EVERY VARIETY OF TOBACCO." The rest of the verbiage is similar to the first box.

Both James J. Mapes and Henry Riell were located on Front Street in New York. New York City directories list Riell at this address between 1822 and 1827. Riell has the further distinction of being accused of misrepresentation and sued by the famous Lorillard tobacco company. The Mapes box is probably from the same period.

The box on the left is very high quality and promotes a saloon in Po'keepsie, New York probably owned by Leander Bantle. Beautifully hand painted in gold lettering on a damask pattern with many coats of varnish, the snuff box is German. Mr. Bantle was a founder of the Germania Singing Society in 1850 which continues today in Poughkeepsie.

The modest black box is later in date and of lesser quality. Edward Hen was an "Importer of Tcco Boxes, Pipes, etc." who worked hard, slept in the store, never married, ate out and occasionally dropped by Wall Street where he dabbled in stocks and bonds and died with $2,000,000 in 1887.

Both these men were clearly up to snuff.

The box above made in Germany and is beautifully hand lettered in gold. The literature tells us that the factory started in 1733 and is the oldest German manufacturer of snuff. By the inscription on the cover, we can date the box itself to 1869. The inner lid has a beautiful transfer of the company's factory buildings on a gold background.

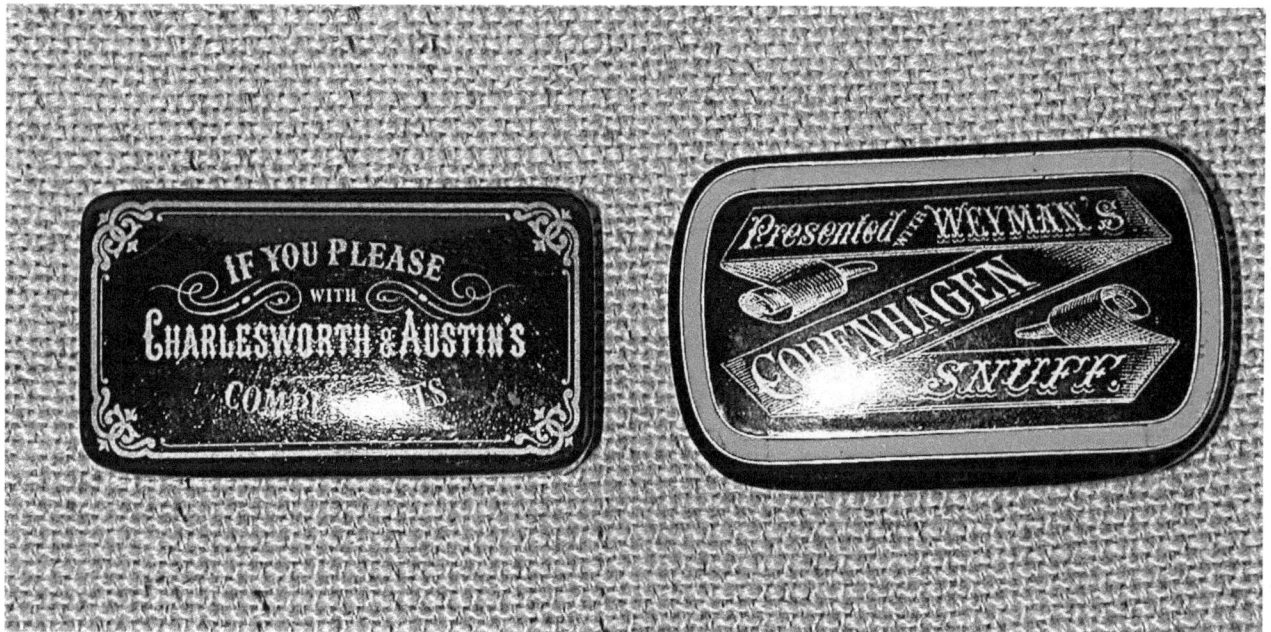

The box on the left is a good example of those advertising boxes given to retailers by manufacturers. Charlesworth & Austin were British manufacturers primarily of cigarettes and also known for their rare tobacco cards. They continued in business into the 1950's. The snuff box is stenciled with gold paint and is typical of later 19th century boxes.

The box on the right is a snuff box advertising the famous Copenhagen snuff. It is also a retailer's box because of the legend clearly states that is "Presented *with* Weyman's Copenhangen Snuff" Gift with purchase- still with us today and standard for perfume promotions. Weyman had a shop in Pittsburg in 1822 and, based upon the success of his snuff blend, the brand continues today. Copenhagen boxes are not rare but this example is a higher quality with the yellow border surrounding the script and having metal inlays.

WAX-PAPER BAGS LIKE THIS WERE QUITE COMMON AT THE TURN OF THE PREVIOUS CENTURY.

FOR CUSTOMERS ORDERING A QUANTITY OF SNUFF OUT OF A LARGER JAR, THE TOBACCONIST COULD JUST WEIGH OUT A BIT AND INSERT IT INTO A BAG, IF THE CUSTOMER DIDN'T HAVE HIS OWN SNUFFBOX.

The author's first encounter with snuff was as a boy when "Dad," the aged, elevator operator, fished the Copenhagen cardboard container out of his uniform pocket and slipped a pinch into his mouth. He explained that it was "candy... but only for men." STE

Simon Handelsman is one of the world's first and foremost authorities on antique snuffboxes. Visit his site, **www.snuffbox.com** *for rare items and free appraisals.*

Win Free Racism!

Did we get your attention? Good!

Now we can talk about this contest.

See, our social media sites are looking pretty dead. Our blog page, our Facebook page and our Youtube videos aren't getting any hits. You would think that we had a circulation of 40 copies or so by the looks of things. This doesn't really inspire confidence in an on-the-fence customer or retailer. Who wants to order three copies of a magazine that only has 46 views of their latest Youtube commercial? (We wouldn't.)

So we're bribing (err... "reaching out to") our readers for help. Watch those videos. Like them. Subscribe to our blog. Connect with us on Facebook and give us a thumbs up for every stupid post we make, just as you do for that hot girl you know from Starbucks who always writes something like "LOL jst walked into a wall" and ends up getting 2,366 'likes.' **Be our pals.**

Each month, we'll choose one lucky (?) poster from each outlet to win a random prize. It could be a year's subscription to the magazine. It could be a rare, out of print back issue. It could be some of the free stuff that we get at conventions and have no use for. (*Ooohh... check out this neat USB Flash Drive carrying pouch they gave us in Louisiana!*) Or it could be cash money! (Actually, no it can't. We're broke.)

If only half of our readership were to connect with us on Facebook or Youtube, we would have thousands of internet "friends," which we all know are more important than the real-life kind. So head over to these sites and get bizaay:

The-Snuff-Takers-Ephemeris

www.youtube.com/user /STephemeris

STephemeris.blogspot.com

Happy Birthday

2012 held some notable milestones for several tobacco brands. Sorry we didn't get a chance to look at them all in detail, but that's what future issues are for!

- **Toque Snuff:** Happy fifth anniversary Roderick!

- **Wilsons of Sharrow:** 275 years of the most consistently well-made snuff is indeed something to be proud of. A British institution surpassed by none other.

- **Ettan Snus and Copenhagen Snuff:** 190 years of heritage and history, they're the reason we started putting snuff in our mouths instead of our noses. Congrats to both!

- **Lucky Strike:** 160th anniversary.

- **Prince Albert:** A big 105 for the US's first national pipe tobacco blend.

- **Garret Snuff Company:** 230 years and still going strong!

- **Key Snuff**: Most recently a Skoal sideline, Key has been running continuously for 75 years. Kudos!

- **Mail Pouch Tobacco:** Although sold locally since 1879 (as West Virginia Mail Pouch Scrap Tobacco), Mail Pouch went countrywide in 1897, becoming the first nationally famous chewing tobacco brand in the US. Happy 115th!

- **And to anyone we may have overlooked, keep on doing what you're doing. We hope to join you on this page in 2110, celebrating the hundredth anniversary of The Snuff Taker's Ephemeris.**

Mariah is 13 years old. She's turned 22 tricks today, and the night's just getting started.

Mariah was just your typical Junior High student. She was pretty and popular. Then she fell in with the wrong crowd.

Bowing to peer pressure, Mariah did her first line of snuff on her 13th birthday. Before she knew it, she was hooked.

Mariah stole from her parents and shoplifted in order to support her addiction. Along the way, she started reading The Ephemeris and learned of new ways to increase her high. But it all came at a terrible price.

Mariah became a streetwalking whore in order to afford the expensive stuff, like Abraxas and Kardus. Men use her and throw her away like a disposable commodity. Her self respect decreases daily.

"Someday," Mariah says, "I'm going to be famous, like the people I read about in the STE. Until then, I'm just going to keep selling my body in order to afford tobacco. These SCHIP taxes are killing me."

Mariah is a snuff taker.

The Ephemeris is her magazine.

Reserve your copy of The Snuff Taker's Ephemeris today at www.snuffmagazine.org.

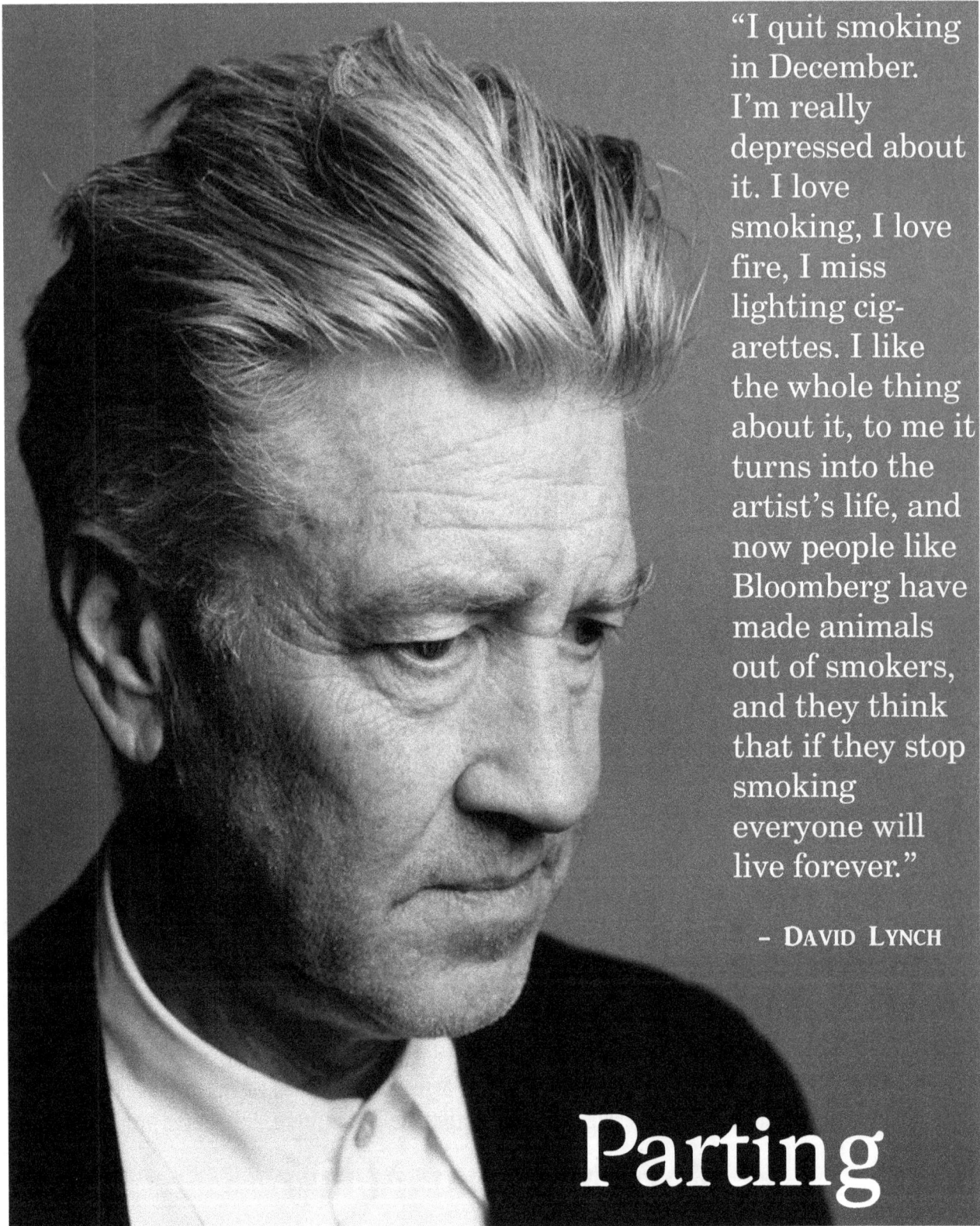

"I quit smoking in December. I'm really depressed about it. I love smoking, I love fire, I miss lighting cigarettes. I like the whole thing about it, to me it turns into the artist's life, and now people like Bloomberg have made animals out of smokers, and they think that if they stop smoking everyone will live forever."

— DAVID LYNCH

Parting Shot

NEXT ISSUE:

MOVING DOWN THE LINE

STE®

© 2012 Lucien Publishing
Fayetteville, NC

Member: Independent Publisher's Trade Guild of North Carolina
"Providing Readers With Books That Matter"